WHAT DID JESUS DO?

A call to return
to the
biblical gospel

RAY COMFORT

genesis
PUBLISHING GROUP

What *Did* Jesus Do? A Call to Return to the Biblical Gospel

Published by
Genesis Publishing Group
2002 Skyline Place
Bartlesville, OK 74006
www.genesis-group.net

Edited by Lynn Copeland

Cover, page design, and production by Genesis Group

Printed in the United States of America

ISBN 0-9749300-3-2

Unless otherwise indicated, Scripture quotations are from the *New King James Version*, © 1979, 1980, 1982 by Thomas Nelson Inc., Publishers, Nashville, Tennessee.

Scripture quotations designated Amplified are from *The Amplified Bible*, © 1965 by Zondervan Publishing House, Grand Rapids, Michigan.

Scripture quotations designated KJV are from the *King James Version*.

To Ben and Melissa Day

CONTENTS

One   The Diagnosis and the Cure 7

Two   What Did Jesus Do? (Part One) *23*

Three   What Did Jesus Do? (Part Two) *39*

Four   What Did Jesus Do? (Part Three) *53*

Five   What Did Paul Do? (Part One) *71*

Six   What Did Paul Do? (Part Two) *93*

Seven   What Did Stephen Do? *107*

Eight   What Did Peter Do? *113*

Nine   What Did James Do? *125*

Ten   What Did John the Baptist Do? *135*

Eleven   What Did Jude Do? *145*

Twelve   What Can *You* Do? *155*

Chapter One

THE DIAGNOSIS AND THE CURE

A television documentary showed a Tibetan peasant woman making her pilgrimage around a sacred mountain. She stopped every few steps to prostrate herself on the rocky soil. She stood to her dust-covered feet, walked a few more paces, and repeated the arduous and painful ritual. She had completed the thirty-two-mile pilgrimage twenty-nine times. Asked why she did it, she smiled sweetly and answered, "We want to be reborn in heaven."

She is not alone in her spiritual philosophy. Much of humanity thinks that by their suffering and self-denial they can enter heaven. They crawl on their bloodied hands and knees, fast from certain foods, cut their bodies, throw their beloved children into the Ganges River, refrain from worldly pleasures, and give money sacrificially to some worthy cause. Many lie on beds of nails, and many more sit on hard pews tormenting themselves under the sound of dull and dry sermons. Very sadly, they think God will consider their suffering or self-denial to be an acceptable sacrifice—a worthy atonement for their sin.

> *It is ignorance of God's moral Law that leaves most of humanity with the delusion that their good works commend them to God.*

However, the payment that they offer God reveals that they lack understanding of the true nature of sin. Like the Jews of old, they seek to establish their own righteousness, *being ignorant of God's righteousness* (see Romans 10:3). This would be like a vicious mass murderer thinking that the good judge will let him go if he simply hands him a day's wages, when the only thing that will satisfy the demands of the law is the finality of the death sentence.

A good judge would be appalled that any sadistic murderer would think he could walk away from justice with a simple payment of a fine. By offering such a menial payment, the criminal shows that he considers that the taking of human life isn't a serious offense. His belief only adds to the nature of his crime.

The Judge of the universe is not satisfied by humanity's self-inflicted suffering. In fact, He is greatly appalled by it. The Bible tells us that the sacrifice of the wicked is an *abomination* to the Lord (see Proverbs 21:27). Even the best that we can offer the Judge is a detestable insult to Him. Our attempts to make any atonement for sin reveal that we don't see our crimes against His Law as being very serious. We trivialize them.

This is why we need the Law (the Ten Commandments) to show us the standard of righteousness that God requires of us. It is ignorance of God's moral Law that leaves most of humanity with the delusion that their good works commend them to God. As long as the peasant woman doesn't know the righteous standard of the Judge she seeks to influence, she will continue to trudge around the sacred hill.

However, the Law reveals that sin is "exceedingly sinful" (see Romans 7:13), and when we see the depth of our sin, we are divorced of any thought that we can make atonement ourselves. It leaves us with nothing but the hope of God's mercy and brings us to the cross of Jesus Christ.

Consider what the Word of God says about the purpose of the Law:

> But we know that the law is good if one uses it lawfully, knowing this: that the law is not made for a righteous person, but for the lawless and insubordinate, for the ungodly and for sinners... (1 Timothy 1:8,9)

These verses state that the Law is good only when it is used "lawfully." It is therefore implied that the Law is bad when it is used unlawfully—for seeking justification or for promoting legalism. It is very clear from Scripture that no one can be made right with God by keeping the moral Law. So what then is the Law's function? Paul tells us:

> Therefore by the deeds of the law no flesh will be justified in His sight, for by the law is the knowledge of sin. (Romans 3:20)

The Law was given by God *to bring the knowledge of sin*, so that a spiritually blind and self-righteous world could see their need for the Savior. This is the lawful use of the Law. Do you know any who are ungodly, who are sinners? The Law was made for them. But when the Law isn't used and a sinner simply makes a "decision for Christ," he lacks understanding of the true nature of sin. He thinks that his good works commend him to God, and he is liable to say "do not touch, do not taste, do not handle"—he becomes legalistic, thinking these things have a role in his salvation.

While many are deceived into thinking they can be justified through the Law or are bound up in legalism, the Law's purpose is to reveal to the world its desperate need of God's mercy. The great biblical commentator Matthew Henry says,

> The abuse which some have made of the Law does not take away the use of it; but, when a divine appointment has been abused, call it back to its right use and take away the abuses, for the Law is still very use-

ful as a rule of life; though we are not under it as under a covenant of works, yet it is good to teach us what is sin and what is duty.[1]

There are many in the Church today who deny this, insisting that the evangelistic use of the Ten Commandments has no basis in Scripture. To those who believe that there are no incidents of the Law's use by the early Church, I present my case in these pages. I do this because I want the Church to see that God gave only one method to reach the lost, and that method is the one we should be using. All other methods are manmade, and are therefore detrimental to the cause of evangelism.

In these pages, we will see that Jesus used the moral Law as He spoke to the lost, and that the use of the Law wasn't confined to the Master Evangelist (as if that weren't enough). My hope is that those who are skeptical will look to Holy Scripture as the final authority on the subject.

While this book explores the application of the Law in evangelism (as do a number of my other publications[2]), it is unique in that it looks specifically at instances where Jesus, Paul, Peter, James, Jude, John the Baptist, and others used

---

[1] Matthew Henry, *Commentary on the Whole Bible* (1721) <http://www.apostolic-churches.net/bible/mhc/mhc54001.htm>.

[2] For a more comprehensive understanding of the importance of using the Law to reach the lost, see *Hell's Best Kept Secret* by Ray Comfort (Whitaker House) and *The Way of the Master* by Kirk Cameron and Ray Comfort (Tyndale House Publishers). See also *How to Win Souls and Influence People* (Bridge-Logos Publishers).

the Law to reach the lost. Throughout the book, to highlight the use of the Ten Commandments, I have footnoted where the Law is mentioned in Scripture. I will also regularly call upon men such as Matthew Henry (perhaps the most respected of Bible commentators), John Wesley, Charles Spurgeon, and others to strengthen my case.

In addition, we will examine biblical instances where they preached the reality of future punishment for those who break the moral Law (a topic that many within the contemporary Church have neglected, in the name of discretion). To make an important point regarding this issue, I have used footnotes to highlight instances of the preaching of future punishment by the One whom we are commanded to imitate.

I will emphasize the importance of preaching the reason that men and women are commanded to repent—because God "has appointed a day in which He will judge the world in righteousness" (Acts 17:30,31). We need to be reminded of these truths in a day in which many within the Church are telling us to forget them.

A Soul-Searching Key

Someone recently put a book into my hands that informed the reader that "the Lord has provided a new tool for sharing." The author then expounded on the "new tool" that God had given him by asking,

> Do you believe it is possible that you could tell them of God's plan of salvation without using "Chris-

tian" words—Jesus, sin, repent, church and God—and still be speaking the Word of God to their hearts?

The author then presented a message of salvation with no reference to repentance or future punishment, calling sin "faults, shortcomings, and bad behavior."

While we must be *culturally* sensitive and gentle when it comes to dealing with the lost, many (including the sincere author of the above book) have taken the thought that we need to be "seeker sensitive" to an extreme, and in so doing have moved far from the biblical example. As J. I. Packer states, "Unless we see our shortcomings in the light of the Law and holiness of God, we do not see them as sin at all."

Failure to speak about the reality of sin and its just consequences will produce dire results. Jim Cymbala, senior pastor of the Brooklyn Tabernacle, says,

> Churches meeting right now, today, are filled with people who are not born again, *but the meetings are such that they will never be pricked in their heart, they will never be disturbed;* they are going to go in and out of church every Sunday, and they will end up making their bed in hell.[3]

With that thought in mind, I would like you to prayerfully read the following e-mail we received from a viewer of "The Way of the Master," a weekly television program that I

---

[3] "The Caller," preached October 10, 2004, tape # PO1492N.

host with Kirk Cameron, on which we teach Christians how to share the gospel biblically:

> God has changed my life through "The Way of the Master." If you would have asked me two weeks ago if I were a Christian, I would have told you (proudly) that I have been one for over 15 years. It wasn't until this week that I really, truly understood that I am a sinner and that I desperately need a Savior. I have been born again.
>
> My heart is breaking for everyone out there who, like me, thinks they are saved, but in reality, are not. If it were not for you telling me, I would have been one of those who would have gone before the Lord and said, "Lord, Lord, did I not prophesy in Your name, and in Your name drive out demons and perform many miracles?" Then He would have told me plainly, "I never knew you. Away from Me, you evildoers!" I would have been cast into the Lake of Fire.
>
> Please keep on saying what you're saying. If I could be deceived into believing that I was saved, anybody could ... I really thought I was going to heaven. Now I *know* I am. Thank you, thank you, thank you again!
>
> —Colleen C.

Tragically, this woman's spiritual experience is typical of *many* in contemporary Christianity. She made a commitment without the knowledge of sin, and the frightening result was that she wasn't saved. Without repentance, there is no salvation. And the lost cannot repent—turn from their sins—and trust in the Savior if they don't know what sin is. Those who make a commitment to Christ but have no knowledge of what sin is will almost certainly have a false conversion. They may do what Christians do, say what Christians say, sing what Christians sing, *but they are not what Christians are*—regenerated by the Holy Spirit. Jesus warned that "many" who called Him "Lord" would be rejected at the gates of heaven and be cast into hell (Matthew 7:21–23).

These "many" people that Jesus spoke of are those "who practice lawlessness" (verse 23). That's something we *must* come to understand. People who are not given the Law may profess faith in Christ, but because of their ignorance of sin they continue to violate the Law of God—they practice lawlessness. Jesus said that there would be *few* genuine conversions and *many* false conversions. These are fearful words, and words we must take seriously if we are serious about reaching this generation.

Could you and I be part of that great multitude who think they are saved when they are not? Have we obeyed the Scriptures and "examined [ourselves] as to whether [we] are in the faith" (2 Corinthians 13:5)? It may be wise to take a moment to go through a short checklist to see if you have evidences of salvation. Don't make the mistake of doing godly things to try to *be* saved. Godly living is the outworking of someone who has *been* saved. If we try to *make* these things happen, we are putting the cart of a supposed godly life before the horse of regeneration. If there is no fruit, there is no root. So go through this short list prayerfully:

- Do you have a deep love and concern that motivates you to reach out to the lost?

- Do you read the Bible every day?

- Do you have a tender conscience before God?

- Do you love other Christians and enjoy their company?

- Do you gossip, or listen to it with glee?

- Do you place your trust in money?

- Do you fail to keep your word, or tell "white" lies?

- Do you take little things that belong to others?

- Do you pray only when things go wrong or when you need or want something?

- Do you consider yourself to be a good person?

Number ten is a soul-searching key that often exposes a false conversion. If we think we are morally good, then something is fundamentally wrong. Jesus said that there is none good but God (see Luke 18:19). If we maintain that we are good, we are implying that Jesus wasn't speaking the truth. Rather, if you think that you are good, it's more than likely that you have never had a true revelation of your own sinful state before God. If that's the case, then there's a possibility that you have had a false conversion, despite your professed godliness. Those who are converted will always agree with Scripture and know experientially that their heart is deceitful and desperately wicked (see Jeremiah 17:9). We are sinful to the very core. In us "nothing good dwells" (Romans 7:18).

If there is even a slight chance that (like the woman whose e-mail we just read), you have never been truly converted, *please* take a moment to go to our website: www.livingwaters.com. Click on "Are You a Good Person?" and go through the test, answering the questions with a tender conscience. You have nothing to lose. Remember, we are talking about your eternity.

If we think we are morally good, then something is fundamentally wrong. Jesus said that there is none good but God.

But I trust that you have already made your calling and election sure, as the Bible exhorts us to do. This will be evidenced by your desire to follow the Lord's command to be a fisher of men (see Matthew 4:19), and when we look at biblical examples of how to "catch" men and women, you will view the Scriptures as the final authority.

As one who has experienced genuine salvation through "repentance toward God and faith toward our Lord Jesus Christ" (Acts 20:21), you will want to take great care to ensure that you don't lead anyone into a false conversion. To share the biblical message of salvation, do what Jesus did in reaching out to the lost—use the Law lawfully.

Check the Soil

The use of the Law in evangelism was something I didn't understand in my first ten years as a Christian. But in 1982 I began to notice this principle being used in Scripture and in history, and implemented it in my own evangelistic efforts. Am I saying that we *must* use the moral Law to bring "the knowledge of sin" every time we share the gospel? Of course not; Jesus didn't.

Scripture tells us that "God resists the proud, but gives grace to the humble" (James 4:6). Those who have a humble heart, who recognize their sin and see their desperate need for God's mercy, will understand the gospel of grace. But the proud and self-righteous—those who proclaim their own goodness (see Proverbs 20:6)—don't see their need for the Savior. They need the Law to show them the righteous standard that God requires.

Biblical evangelism therefore follows the principle of "Law to the proud, and grace to the humble." If someone is proud and self-righteous—like the self-righteous man who ran to the Savior[4] and asked how to be saved—we must do what Jesus did. We should give him the Law to show him the nature of sin. If he is humble of heart (already possessing the knowledge of sin), such as in the case of Nicodemus, then we should do what Jesus did and give him grace.

It is as simple as sowing seed. A wise farmer always checks the soil *before* he plants seed. If the soil has stones,

---

[4]   We will look closely at this and other incidents in the book.

he removes them. If it is hard, he breaks it up. He knows that if he wants to successfully grow a crop, he must properly prepare the soil *before* he sows the precious seed. That's the principle behind the evangelistic use of the Law: "Law before grace."

In the same way, a wise doctor doesn't give a cure to a patient who has no understanding that he has a serious disease. If the doctor doesn't show him the severe nature of his illness (that, left untreated, it will kill him), the patient won't appreciate the cure. Left in ignorance about the seriousness of his plight, the patient may neglect taking the cure, and therefore die. So the good doctor looks his ignorant patient in the eye, and takes the time to thorough-

> *The Law and the gospel should never be separated. They are made for each other. One is the diagnosis; the other is the cure.*

ly explain the malady and its terrible consequence. He doesn't deliberately avoid certain words that may alarm his patient. He *wants* to alarm him.

God's Law alerts the sinner to the malady of sin. It widens his complacent eyes and causes alarm. It brings the diagnosis proving to the patient that he is terribly and terminally diseased. It helps him to understand sin and its result, so that he will then appropriate the cure of the cross.

It is because of this that the Law and the gospel should never be separated. They are made for each other. One is the diagnosis; the other is the cure. The diagnosis without the cure is futile. The cure with the diagnosis is senseless. The Law exposes the disease; the gospel treats it.

John Wesley says,

> The very first end of the Law [is], namely, convicting men of sin; awakening those who are still asleep on the brink of hell... The ordinary method of God is to convict sinners by the Law, and that only. The gospel is not the means which God hath ordained, or which our Lord Himself used, for this end.

Think of God's Law as an extension cord that is plugged into the power of Heaven. The gospel is a light bulb. Without the Law, the gospel is powerless; it leaves the lost in the dark about their sin and its deadly consequences. The gospel—the news that Jesus died on the cross for our sins—gives no light to the mind of sinners whose understanding is "darkened, being alienated from the life of God, because of the ignorance that is in them, because of the blindness of their heart" (Ephesians 4:18). The god of this world has blinded their minds "lest the light of the gospel of the glory of Christ, who is the image of God, should shine on them" (2 Corinthians 4:4).

The message of the cross is therefore foolishness to a world that is perishing (see 1 Corinthians 1:18). However, once the gospel is connected to the Law, it becomes the power of God to salvation. The Law gives the gospel its light—it enlightens the lost about the nature of sin and shows them their desperate need for the Savior.

I have seen this happen thousands of times, and once you see the effect of both the Law and the gospel working together, you will have your eyes opened also. You will say (like many others I have heard from), "How could I have not seen this before!" Later in this book, we will look at how you can implement the Law in the gospel presentation.

Charles Spurgeon said, "There is no point on which men make greater mistakes than on the relation which exists between the Law and the gospel." Therefore, in the next chapter, we will begin to examine what Jesus did when He reached out to the lost, so that we can follow in His footsteps.

Chapter Two

WHAT DID JESUS DO? (PART ONE)

S even hundred years before the birth of Christ, the Scriptures told us that God would magnify the Law and make it honorable (see Isaiah 42:21). During the time of Christ, we see a dishonored Law—a Law that had been made void by the traditions of men (see Mark 7:6–13). It had been stripped of its power to bring the knowledge of sin (see Romans 3:20) and to show sin to be exceedingly sinful (see Romans 7:13).

The religious leaders had desecrated that which had been entrusted to them. They warped its holy precepts and twisted the strictness of its ordinances. They nullified its incredible power to do that for which it was intended. In neglecting the "weightier matters of the law" (Matthew 23:23), they instead strained at gnats and swallowed camels, limiting its precepts to a mere outward piety. They worshiped God in vain because they had laid aside the Commandment of God and instead taught the commandments of men (see Mark 7:7–9).

But Jesus reminded them of what they had neglected, straightened what they had made crooked, and magnified what they demeaned. He also re-established the Law's permanency. This was the Law that God Himself had written in stone. Despite man's amendments, it would not change—not one jot or tittle. Instead, it was the stony heart of man that had to change.

"Without thorough conviction of sin, men may seem to come to Jesus and follow Him for a season, but they will soon fall away and return to the world."

It was at this time that the Law was magnified and made honorable by the Messiah, particularly through the Sermon on the Mount. As we will see, Jesus opened up the Law's true nature for a purpose.

In his book *Holiness*, J. C. Ryle writes:

> Let us expound and beat out the Ten Commandments, and show the length, and breadth, and depth, and height of their requirements. This is the way of

our Lord in the Sermon on the Mount. We cannot do better than follow His plan. We may depend on it: men will never come to Jesus, and stay with Jesus, and live for Jesus, unless they really know why they are to come, and what is their need. Those whom the Spirit draws to Jesus are those whom the Spirit has convinced of sin. Without thorough conviction of sin, men may seem to come to Jesus and follow Him for a season, but they will soon fall away and return to the world.

The Spirituality of the Law

Let's look at how Jesus took the time to magnify the Law and make it honorable. In Matthew 5:17–19, He told His hearers that He came not to destroy the Law but to fulfill it, and that if they would practice and teach God's Law, they would be considered great in the kingdom of heaven. He then opened up the spiritual nature of the Law through the Sermon on the Mount, explaining that outward observance of the Commandments was not enough. God desires "truth in the inward parts" (see Psalm 51:6). He will judge down to our thought life, intent, and motives.

Some maintain that Jesus wasn't referring to the Ten Commandments when He used the word "law." They believe it is a general reference to the Old Testament or to "the revealed will of God." While it is true that the word "law" is often used in Scripture to refer to the Old Testament, it is clear that Jesus is speaking here of the Decalogue (the moral Law—the Ten Commandments). He refers to both "the

Law" and "these commandments," and He then specifically names two of the Commandments as He opens up their spiritual nature:

> "You have heard that it was said to those of old, 'You shall not murder,[5] and whoever murders will be in danger of the judgment.'[6] But I say to you that whoever is angry with his brother without a cause shall be in danger of the judgment.[7] And whoever says to his brother, 'Raca!' shall be in danger of the council. But whoever says, 'You fool!' shall be in danger of hell fire.[8]... You have heard that it was said to those of old, 'You shall not commit adultery.'[9] But I say to you that whoever looks at a woman to lust for her has already committed adultery with her in his heart." (Matthew 5:21,22,27,28)

Jesus declares that even those who have not committed the act of murder may not be innocent in God's eyes. He sees the thoughts and intents of the heart, and declares that whoever is angry without cause is guilty of transgressing the Sixth Commandment. The Bible further adds that whoever hates his brother is a murderer (see 1 John 3:15).

In commenting on the Law's spiritual nature, Matthew Henry says,

---

[5] Eighth Commandment.
[6] Future punishment.
[7] Future punishment.
[8] Future punishment.
[9] Seventh Commandment.

Herein is the Law of God above all other laws, that it is a spiritual law. Other laws may forbid compassing and imagining, which are treason in the heart, but cannot take cognizance thereof, unless there be some overt act; but the Law of God takes notice of the iniquity regarded in the heart, though it go no further.

Jesus then addressed the serious nature of the sin of lust, by warning of its terrible consequences:

"If your right eye causes you to sin, pluck it out and cast it from you; for it is more profitable for you that one of your members perish, than for your whole body to be cast into hell.[10] And if your right hand causes you to sin, cut if off and cast it from you; for it is more profitable for you that one of your members perish, than for your whole body to be cast into hell."[11] (Matthew 5:29,30)

If your eye is roaming uncontrolled and feeding the heart with unlawful images, it would be better to pluck it out and cast it from you, than to be cast into hell forever. If your hand is turning the pages of a pornographic magazine, using a mouse to surf porn websites, or pressing the TV remote buttons to view a sexually explicit program, it would be better to have no hands and be unable to sin than to be cast into hell. What powerful imagery Jesus used! While some people might consider such talk to be negative,

---

[10] Future punishment.
[11] Future punishment.

offensive, or insensitive, it is the truth, and Jesus' motivation for speaking the truth was love.

The Master Teacher magnified the Law further by opening up His listeners' understanding of the Ninth Commandment ("You shall not bear false witness"):

> "Again you have heard that it was said to those of old, 'You shall not swear falsely, but shall perform your oaths to the Lord.' But I say to you, do not swear at all: neither by heaven, for it is God's throne; nor by the earth, for it is His footstool; nor by Jerusalem, for it is the city of the great King. Nor shall you swear by your head, because you cannot make one hair white or black. But let your 'Yes' be 'Yes,' and your 'No,' 'No.' For whatever is more than these is from the evil one." (Matthew 5:33–37)

Here Jesus is saying that we must be trustworthy and have integrity in all that we say and do, demonstrating truthfulness not just in our words but also in our actions.

Sermon Climax

Jesus was using the Law to destroy any thought His listeners may have of self-atonement, steering them toward the righteousness that comes only by faith. He later instructed them, "Seek first the kingdom of God and *His* righteousness" (Matthew 6:33, emphasis added). As we talk to the lost, this should also be our aim, with the help of God: to destroy the deception of self-righteousness. How do we do that? By doing what Jesus did. He revealed the spiritual nature of the Law—that we are to abide not just by the *letter* of the Law, but by the *spirit* of the Law.

We must tell sinners that God considers lust to be adultery and hatred to be murder, because if we don't, they may make a profession of faith and still give themselves to hatred and lust. They will continue to "practice lawlessness." If we are to be true and faithful in our witness, we mustn't hesitate to tell sinners to pluck out their eye if it causes them to sin, and that it would be better to enter heaven blind than to go to hell with both eyes. We must show them how far we have all fallen short of the glory of God's holy standard—to love one's neighbor as oneself, for love is the fulfillment of the Law (Romans 13:10).

Jesus climaxed this part of His preaching with a statement that must have left His hearers speechless, which was no doubt His intention. The Law's function is that "every mouth may be stopped" (see Romans 3:19). He said,

> "Therefore you shall be perfect, just as your Father in heaven is perfect." (Matthew 5:48)

Some Bible commentators believe Jesus didn't really mean "perfect" here, because that would require that we be "without defect, flawless." Instead, they think He was telling us to be *mature*. If that were true, then He would be saying, "Therefore be mature, just as your Father in heaven is mature." However, calling God "mature" implies that He was once immature—a thought that is contrary to Scripture.

Malachi 3:6 tells us that God never changes. He has always been perfect and doesn't need to mature. His way is perfect (2 Samuel 22:31); His work is perfect (Deuteronomy 32:4); His knowledge is perfect (Job 37:16); His will is perfect (Romans 12:2).

Who can justify himself in God's sight if we are commanded to be perfect? We are all speechless *once we understand what God expects of us*. None of us is perfect. Therefore, our sinful mouths are stopped and we have nothing to say in our defense.

D. L. Moody explains:

> Ask Paul why [the Law] was given. Here is his answer, "That every mouth may be stopped, and all the world may become guilty before God" (Romans 3:19). The Law stops every man's mouth. I can always tell a man who is near the kingdom of God; his mouth is stopped. This, then, is why God gives us the Law— to show us ourselves in our true colors.

God's Law is perfect, and if we are not perfect on the Day of Judgment, we will perish. This moral perfection must and will search out every moral imperfection. That's why Paul says that we are to warn every man and present every man "perfect" in Christ (see Colossians 1:28).

When a man told Jesus that he had kept the Law from his youth, Jesus began His response by saying, "If you want to be perfect..." (Matthew 19:21). Jesus said this because the Law demands perfection—in thought, word, and deed.

Scripture tells us that the man went away sorrowful. Understanding our need for perfection dashes any false hope we might have of becoming "good enough" in God's eyes. All who look into the mirror of the Law should be sorrowful. The Law can do nothing for us but show us our moral deficiency before God. It can't make us perfect, but it can point us to the blood of the Savior that can. The Bible tells us, "For the law made nothing perfect; on the other hand, there is the bringing in of a better hope, through which we draw near to God" (Hebrews 7:19).

The Law can do nothing for us but show us our moral deficiency before God. It can't make us perfect, but it can point us to the blood of the Savior that can.

Again, when we look into the perfect Law of liberty (see James 1:25), all it does is show us that we stand imperfect before a perfect and holy Creator. It simply and justly points its holier-than-thou finger and accuses, denounces, and condemns. It leaves us without hope, and drives us to the realization that there is no salvation for sinful humanity outside of the mercy of God.

Jesus then preached the essence of the First of the Ten Commandments ("You shall have no other gods before Me"):

"No one can serve two masters; for either he will hate the one and love the other, or else he will be loyal to the one and despise the other. You cannot serve God and mammon." (Matthew 6:24)

In pointing to the First Commandment, Jesus spoke of His own worthiness of honor. Because He was God manifest in the flesh (1 Timothy 3:16), the Law required that *He* be first in our affections:

"He who loves father or mother more than Me is not worthy of Me. And he who loves son or daughter more than Me is not worthy of Me. And he who does not take his cross and follow after Me is not worthy of Me." (Matthew 10:37,38)

The Fear of the Lord

To understand the importance of this "perfect Law of liberty," let's look for a moment at Psalm 19, which is a treatise of the moral Law.

The law of the LORD is perfect, converting the soul; the testimony of the LORD is sure, making wise the simple; the statutes of the LORD are right, rejoicing the heart; the commandment of the LORD is pure, enlightening the eyes; the fear of the LORD is clean, enduring forever; the judgments of the LORD are true and righteous altogether. More to be desired are they than gold, yea, than much fine gold; sweeter also than honey and the honeycomb. Moreover by them Your servant is warned, and in keeping them there is great

reward. Who can understand his errors? Cleanse me
from secret faults. (Psalm 19:7–12)

Scripture tells us that God's Law is perfect and actually
converts the soul (verse 7). Once the soul is transformed by
the power of the gospel, the heart rejoices with joy unspeakable. As we have seen, the Commandment of the Lord
has the effect of "enlightening the eyes" (verse 8). The simple are made wise by being given understanding of, among
others things, the final and terrible result of sin. The Law
therefore produces in sinners the most necessary virtue,
"the fear of the Lord"—"by them Your servant is warned"
(verse 11). This not only causes them to *depart* from sin,
but it *keeps* them from the power of sin. The Commandments are therefore more to be desired than "much fine
gold" (verse 10). Unregenerate, blind, sinful people cannot
understand their errors. The Law shows them the error of
their ways, leading them to cry out to God, "Cleanse me
from secret faults" (verse 12).

This perfect Law converts the soul by enlightening sinners, producing the fear of the Lord, and warning them of
their errors. This is no doubt why Jesus took the time to
magnify the Law and make it honorable. He didn't hesitate
to speak of hell as the just punishment for those who violate the moral Law of a holy God.

Tragically, many modern preachers have strayed far from
preaching about sin, righteousness, and judgment, despite
the fact that we are commanded to pursue the biblical ex-

ample (see 1 Corinthians 11:1). Instead, they furnish a soft pillow for sleeping sinners, going to great lengths *not* to awaken them to the reality of sin. Words are crafted as to not alarm, by painting the character of God as one of a philanthropic father figure. It is not often that we hear preachers putting the fear of God in the hearts of their hearers, as Jesus did. He warned:

> "Do not fear those who kill the body but cannot kill the soul. But rather fear Him who is able to destroy both soul and body in hell."[12] (Matthew 10:28)

> "But I say to you that for every idle word men may speak, they will give account of it in the day of judgment.[13] For by your words you will be justified, and by your words you will be condemned." (Matthew 12:36,37)

Jesus said that we shouldn't fear those who can kill the body. Think about that for a moment. How could someone kill your body? Perhaps a ruthless murderer could attack you with a fifteen-inch stainless steel serrated meat knife, plunging it into your chest with such force that it comes out in the middle of your back. Imagine seeing the unspeakably horrific sight of warm blood surging from your chest in your final seconds of life. Such thoughts are horrendous! But Jesus told us not to fear the man who would

---

[12] Future punishment.
[13] Future punishment.

do such a thing. Don't fear him? That scenario doesn't make me *fearful*, it *terrifies* me, and that terror comes from my God-given instinct to survive. Yet Jesus said not to fear him who can kill the body. What did He mean?

The Master Teacher often used hyperbole in His teachings. In contrasting love with hate, gnats with camels, hot with cold, He used extremes to emphasize a point. This, in essence, is what He was saying: Does the thought of having a sharp knife thrust through your chest scare you? That fear is nothing compared to the unspeakable horror of facing the wrath of Almighty God on the Day of Judgment.

Jesus said that it would be better to drown with a millstone tied around your neck than to face God's punishment (Matthew 18:6). The Bible warns that it is a fearful thing to fall into the hands of the living God (Hebrews 10:31). Why then doesn't the world fear God? Because we haven't told them to. Rather than following Jesus' example, we may be guilty of feeding them a benevolent image of God's character with the message that Jesus will provide peace, joy, love, fulfillment, and lasting happiness. To many, the gospel is nothing more than a heavenly offer to give us a happier life than the one we have without God.

Our churches today frequently teach principles of daily living, instructing people on how to find victory over life's many problems, make their marriage work, raise their kids, etc. Modern preachers often talk about anything but sin, righteousness, and judgment—thereby removing the very elements that produce the fear of the Lord.

The psalmist writes, "My flesh trembles for fear of You, and I am afraid of Your judgments" (Psalm 119:120). God's Law will be unrelenting on the Day of Judgment. It will be like the noble sheriff who tenaciously follows the winding and dusty trail of a vicious murderer. He will go to the ends of the earth to bring the criminal to justice. The Law will pursue the crooked and dark path of sin right down to the intents of the sinful human heart, to the thoughts and motives, to every idle word spoken, and will bring to light every secret thing, whether it is good or evil (see Ecclesiastes 12:14). No one will outrun the Law.

Why should sinners be made to fear God? Is the motive to simply terrify them for some sort of perverted pleasure? Of course not. Jesus didn't speak of these things because He despised the lost and wanted them to perish. His motive was the opposite. God loves sinners and doesn't want anyone to perish. The Scriptures tell us, "Faithful are the wounds of a friend, but the kisses of an enemy are deceitful" (Proverbs 27:6). Talk about the surety of future punishment *is* wounding, and it is therefore easy to shy away from such speech. But if we refuse to "wound" sinners with the truth, and instead caress them with non-offensive words, we are betrayers of the ultimate trust.

Listen to Charles Spurgeon's words of warning:

> Sir surgeon, you are too delicate to tell the man that he is ill! You hope to heal the sick without their knowing it. You therefore flatter them; and what hap-

pens? They laugh at you; they dance upon their own graves. At last they die! Your delicacy is cruelty; your flatteries are poisons; you are a murderer. Shall we keep men in a fool's paradise? Shall we lull them into soft slumbers from which they will awake in hell? Are we to become helpers of their damnation by our smooth speeches? In the name of God we will not.

If we care about the lost, we will not hesitate to speak to them about sin, righteousness, and judgment...the way Jesus did. In the next chapter we will continue to look at examples of how Jesus used the moral Law to reach the lost.

Chapter Three

WHAT DID JESUS DO?
(PART TWO)

We live in days of rampant hypocrisy. As a result of our failure to give people the knowledge of sin and its consequences, there are many who profess faith in Christ but whose lives say otherwise. Without a proper fear of the Lord, they have a form of godliness but deny its power in their lives. Millions of people fall into this category, so how should we awaken them? Let's look at how the Master Evangelist used the moral Law to reprove the hypocrites of His day. Jesus said,

"Why do you also transgress the commandment of God because of your tradition? For God commanded, saying, 'Honor your father and mother';[14] and, 'He who curses father or mother, let him be put to death.' ... Hypocrites! Well did Isaiah prophesy about you, saying: 'These people draw near to Me with their mouth, and honor Me with their lips, but their heart is far from Me. And in vain they worship Me, teaching as doctrines the commandments of men.'" (Matthew 15:3,4,7–9)

These are not the gentle, affirming words of life enhancement that can be heard in many churches today. Why would Jesus speak so harshly? Because He wanted to alarm those who were self-righteous, to awaken them to their true state. He used the Law to bring the knowledge of sin, telling His listeners that they have transgressed the "commandment of God," specifically referencing the Fifth Commandment.

If we care about the salvation of the lost, we will want to awaken them and bring them to true repentance.

Again, Jesus didn't avoid words that might offend His hearers. When told that His words had offended the Pharisees, He emphasized the certainty of future punishment (verses 12–14). He then explained to His disciples what defiles a man, giving them a list of sins and where they originate. Jesus lists several

---

14   Fifth Commandment.

of the Commandments, clearly showing that "sin is transgression of the Law" (1 John 3:4, KJV):

> "For out of the heart proceed evil thoughts, murders,[15] adulteries,[16] fornications,[17] thefts,[18] false witness,[19] blasphemies.[20] These are the things which defile a man, but to eat with unwashed hands does not defile a man." (Matthew 15:19,20)

Jesus continually honored the Law and opened up its spiritual nature to give understanding to the self-righteous Pharisees. God only knows how many of them were awakened by the knowledge that they had sinned, and found themselves among the three thousand saved souls on the Day of Pentecost.

If we care about the salvation of the lost, we will want to awaken them and bring them to true repentance. Rather than sharing an inoffensive gospel that creates false converts (hypocrites), we must follow the biblical principle of "Law to the proud, grace to the humble." Let's look at examples of Jesus addressing individuals to see how He dealt with the self-righteous and the humble of heart.

---

[15] Sixth Commandment.
[16] Seventh Commandment.
[17] Seventh Commandment (see 1 Timothy 1:8–10).
[18] Eighth Commandment.
[19] Ninth Commandment.
[20] Third Commandment.

Jesus and the Rich Young Ruler

We see Jesus use the Ten Commandments in Mark chapter 10 with what seemed to be an earnest young man who came running to Him. The man humbly knelt down, complemented Jesus on being "good," and asked how he could obtain everlasting life. He appears to be an ideal audience for the gospel message. Let's look at the Scriptures to see how Jesus responded:

> Now as He was going out on the road, one came running, knelt before Him, and asked Him, "Good Teacher, what shall I do that I may inherit eternal life?" So Jesus said to him, "Why do you call Me good? No one is good but One, that is, God. You know the commandments: Do not commit adultery,[21] Do not murder,[22] Do not steal,[23] Do not bear false witness,[24] Do not defraud, Honor your father and your mother."[25] And he answered and said to Him, "Teacher, all these things I have kept from my youth." Then Jesus, looking at him, loved him, and said to him, "One thing you lack: Go your way, sell whatever you have and give to the poor, and you will have treasure in heaven; and come, take up the cross, and follow Me." (Mark 10:17–22)

---

[21] Seventh Commandment.
[22] Sixth Commandment.
[23] Eighth Commandment.
[24] Ninth Commandment.
[25] Fifth Commandment.

The man's earnest and humble heart would seem to make him a prime candidate as a potential convert. Modern evangelism would give this man the message of God's love and have him pray a "sinner's prayer." And why *shouldn't* we do that, since it has worked for multitudes? *Because it's not what Jesus did in such a case.* He didn't share the message of God's grace. Instead, He reproved the man's understanding of the word "good" by opening up God's standard of goodness. He used the Law to expose the man's hidden sin: this man was a transgressor of the First of the Ten Commandments. His money was his god, and one cannot serve both God and money.

Love is concerned with seeing a genuine conversion, rather than seeking a sense of accomplishment in leading someone in a sinner's prayer whose heart isn't right with God.

Verse 21 reveals that it was *love* that motivated the Savior to speak in this way to this rich young man. Love is concerned with seeing a genuine conversion, rather than seeking a sense of accomplishment in leading someone in a sinner's prayer whose heart isn't right with God.

Jesus and a Scribe

Here is an incident of Jesus bringing out the essence of the Law. Consider His answer to a scribe who asked Him a question:

Then one of the scribes came, and having heard them reasoning together, perceiving that He had answered them well, asked Him, "Which is the first commandment of all?" Jesus answered him, "The first of all the commandments is: 'Hear, O Israel, the LORD our God, the LORD is one. And you shall love the LORD your God with all your heart, with all your soul, with all your mind, and with all your strength.' This is the first commandment. And the second, like it, is this: 'You shall love your neighbor as yourself.' There is no other commandment greater than these."

So the scribe said to Him, "Well said, Teacher. You have spoken the truth, for there is one God, and there is no other but He. And to love Him with all the heart, with all the understanding, with all the soul, and with all the strength, and to love one's neighbor as oneself, is more than all the whole burnt offerings and sacrifices."

Now when Jesus saw that he answered wisely, He said to him, "You are not far from the kingdom of God." (Mark 12:28–34)

Those who love God and man will not steal, lie, murder, commit adultery, covet, etc.; therefore, love is the fulfillment of the Law (see Romans 13:10). How we have failed to keep these, the greatest of Commandments! The Bible says that there is none who seeks after God (see Romans 3:11). The Law reveals how much we have sinned, and shows our terrible ingratitude to God for life itself. How many of us can look into the face of the Law and say that we love our neighbor as much as we love ourselves? We have trouble loving our loved ones as much as we love ourselves, let alone total strangers.

D. L. Moody, echoing the sentiment of Jesus' words in Mark 12:34, said,

> I can always tell a man who is near the kingdom of God; his mouth is stopped. This, then, is why God gives us the Law—to show us ourselves in our true colors.

When a man understands the requirements of the Law, it moves him closer to the cross. The Law is the schoolmaster that God uses to guide us to the Savior (see Galatians 3:24).

Jesus and the Proud Lawyer

A lawyer, a professing expert on God's Law, asked Jesus how to find everlasting life. Again, we may consider this a perfect opportunity to tell the person of God's grace. But watch how Jesus uses the Law to bring the knowledge of sin:

> And behold, a certain lawyer stood up and tested Him, saying, "Teacher, what shall I do to inherit eternal life?" He said to him, "What is written in the law? What is your reading of it?" So he answered and said, "'You shall love the LORD your God with all your heart, with all your soul, with all your strength, and with all your mind,' and 'your neighbor as yourself.'" And He said to him, "You have answered rightly; do this and you will live." But he, wanting to justify him-

self, said to Jesus, "And who is my neighbor?" (Luke 10:25–29)

This man was arrogant and self-righteous—he stood up and brazenly tested the Savior. Charles Spurgeon said, "A brazen face and a broken heart never go together." This lawyer needed to be humbled by the Law in which he professed expertise, so Jesus gave him its demands—we are commanded to love our neighbor as much as we love ourselves. If you read the full narrative (verses 30–37), you will see that Jesus told him the story of the good Samaritan to illustrate the spirit of the Law, showing the man how far he had fallen short of its requirements.

Jesus pointed this proud man to the Law of God so that he could recognize his *personal* sin. The Law brought "the knowledge of sin" (Romans 3:20), seen in the fact that he tried to justify his guilt.

The Law was made not for the righteous but for sinners (see 1 Timothy 1:9), for those who are trusting in their good works to commend them to God. God gave us the sharp needle of His Law so that we might burst the bubble of self-righteous, proud humanity. In John 7:19, Jesus again used the Law to bring the knowledge of sin to His hearers, telling them that they had not kept its precepts:

"Did not Moses give you the law, yet none of you keeps the law? Why do you seek to kill[26] Me?"

---

[26] Sixth Commandment.

When Jesus spoke to the proud religious leaders in John 5:45–47, He told them that the Law of Moses accused them:

> "Do not think that I shall accuse you to the Father; there is one who accuses you; Moses, in whom you trust. For if you believed Moses, you would believe Me; for he wrote about Me. But if you do not believe his writings, how will you believe My words?"

Jesus wasn't saying that they trusted in the person of Moses, but in what Moses said. The Law of Moses *accused* them of sin. Those who are humbled, because they understand that they have sinned by transgressing the Law of Moses, are prepared to believe and trust in the words of Jesus. Only then will they be receptive to the message of God's grace.

Jesus and the Pharisees

In Luke 16:14–18, when Jesus addressed the covetous Pharisees, did He preach the cross? Did He give them the message of God's love? No. Once again, He used the Law to bring the knowledge of sin:

> Now the Pharisees, who were lovers of money [covetous],[27] also heard all these things, and they derided Him. And He said to them, "You are those who justify yourselves before men, but God knows your hearts. For what is highly esteemed among men is an

---

[27] Tenth Commandment.

abomination in the sight of God. The law and the prophets were until John. Since that time the kingdom of God has been preached, and everyone is pressing into it.[28] And it is easier for heaven and earth to pass away than for one tittle of the law to fail. Whoever divorces his wife and marries another commits adultery;[29] and whoever marries her who is divorced from her husband commits adultery."

Like many today, the Pharisees were coveting not just material goods, but apparently also their neighbor's wife. Divorce has become common and acceptable in contemporary society. In the last thirty years, America's divorce rate has skyrocketed from 23 per thousand to 400–500 per thousand in 2004.[30] According to the U.S. Census Bureau, there are 5.3 million people who "cohabit."[31]

But the Seventh Commandment doesn't take a back seat when lust drives a person toward another spouse. It stands as a severe warning of an impending collision. Jesus used the Law to show us that what we accept as normal isn't acceptable to God—it is an abomination—and we sin against Him when we commit adultery.

---

[28] The Law had been doing its job in Israel, and when John the Baptist preached the forgiveness of sins, multitudes flocked to him for baptism, "pressing into the kingdom."

[29] Seventh Commandment.

[30] *More*, March 2004, "Shacking Up is Back," p. 105.

[31] U.S. Census Bureau, Census 2000 Summary File 4 <http://factfinder.census.gov>.

Jesus and the Adulterous Woman

We are told in John chapter 8 of a woman who was guilty of breaking the Seventh Commandment. The scribes and the Pharisees dragged her into the midst of a crowd, saying that she had been caught in the very act of adultery. It was a "smoking gun" trial. There was no doubt as to her guilt, so it was merely a matter of carrying out the punishment demanded by the Law. It obviously takes two to tango, but there is no mention of the guilty male. It would seem that the accusers were both hypocritical and partial in their condemnation.

They told Jesus that the Law *demanded* her death, and they wanted to know if He would uphold its harsh precepts and call for her execution by stoning (verse 5). They were neither humble nor sincere in their question, but were proud and self-righteous (verse 6). They needed the Law to bring them the knowledge of sin, to humble their proud hearts and show them that they too were guilty before God.

Here we see Jesus allowing the Law to do its wonderful work:

> Then the scribes and Pharisees brought to Him a woman caught in adultery.[32] And when they had set her in the midst, they said to Him, "Teacher, this woman was caught in adultery, in the very act. Now Moses, in the law, commanded us that such should be stoned. But what do You say?" This they said, testing

---

[32] Seventh Commandment.

Him, that they might have something of which to accuse Him.

But Jesus stooped down and wrote on the ground with His finger, as though He did not hear. So when they continued asking Him, He raised Himself up and said to them, "He who is without sin among you, let him throw a stone at her first." And again He stooped down and wrote on the ground. Then those who heard it, being convicted by their conscience, went out one by one, beginning with the oldest even to the last. And Jesus was left alone, and the woman standing in the midst. (John 8:3–9)

The wrath of the Law brought this sinful woman to the feet of the Savior. That's its function—to condemn the sinner. Some may say that Christians are not to *condemn* anyone. But the Law reveals to the sinner that he is "condemned already" (see John 3:18). The Law shows him his danger and therefore his desperate need for the Savior. It acts as a schoolmaster, giving the necessary knowledge that will bring the sinner to Christ (see Galatians 3:24).

Jonathan Edwards says of the lost, "By a clear discovery of the connection between their sin and God's wrath, they are sensible of their danger of hell... The threatenings of the law make them afraid indeed, that God will punish sins."

The Law did a great work for this woman. It called for her blood. Its terrible threat of death by stoning no doubt horrified her, and brought her trembling in guilt. Guilt and fear go hand-in-hand. If she wasn't guilty, she need not have feared. But having been caught in the act of adultery, she couldn't deny her culpability. Her mouth was stopped and she could offer no excuses. She no doubt began to labor and become heavy laden under the weight of the Law's threatening. Its burdensome weight forced her to the ground at the feet of the Savior.

That is the lowly state in which a guilty sinner *should* come to the Savior. Jesus said, "Come to Me, all you who labor and are heavy laden" (Matthew 11:28). This is not an invitation to come to Jesus because we are heavy laden with troubles, as modern preachers so often say. Listen to what Matthew Henry said about laboring and being heavy laden:

> All those, and those only, are invited to rest in Christ, that are sensible of sin as a burden, and groan under it; that are not only convinced of the evil of sin, of their own sin, but are contrite in soul for it; that are really sick of their sins, weary of the service of the world and of the flesh; that see their state sad and dangerous by reason of sin, and are in pain and fear about it, as Ephraim (Jer. 31:18–20), the prodigal (Luke 15:17), the publican (Luke 18:13), Peter's hearers (Acts 2:37), Paul (Acts 9:4,6,9), the jailer (Acts 16:29,30). This is a necessary preparative for pardon and peace. The Comforter must first convince (John 16:8); I have torn and then will heal.[33]

---

[33] Matthew Henry, *Commentary on the Whole Bible* <www.apostolic-churches.net/bible/mhc/matthew/11.html>.

Some think that when Jesus wrote with His finger as though He hadn't heard them, He listed the accusers' sins. Others believe that He wrote out the Ten Commandments. Whatever He inscribed, it certainly stopped their self-righteous mouths, humbled them, and they unquestionably became aware of their sin. The Bible tells us that their consciences suddenly accused them, and they left, beginning with the eldest.

No one was left to accuse this woman, and when you and I come to the Savior, the Law can no longer condemn us. We are left standing alone with Jesus. He is our Savior, our only hope...and those who realize what they have been saved from will go their way and sin no more.

Chapter Four

WHAT DID JESUS DO? (PART THREE)

Although Jesus used the Commandments when reaching out to the lost, some argue that He did so only because He was dealing with self-righteous Jews—those who were "under the law." Since obedience to the Law was the Jews' hope of salvation, some believe that Jesus was turning their own confidence against them by citing the legal foundation of the Old Covenant, "do this and live" (Luke 10:26–28). This argument insinuates that the Law was given only to deal with self-righteous Jews—that the

53

Gentiles (non-Jewish people) had some superior knowledge and did not need the Law to show them their sin.

However, Scripture is clear that both Jews and Gentiles lack understanding: "There is none who understands..." (Romans 3:11). Both therefore need the Law to bring the knowledge of sin. When Paul said, "I would not have known sin except through the Law" (Romans 7:7), he didn't add, "This is because I was a self-righteous Jew. Had I been a self-righteous Gentile, I would not have needed the Law to show me the nature of sin." Scripture tells us for whom the Law was given:

> Now we know that whatever the law says, it says to those who are under the law, that *every* mouth may be stopped, and *all the world* may become guilty before God. (Romans 3:19, emphasis added)

Clearly, the Law is for everyone. Scripture tells us that the Jews have an advantage over the Gentiles because they were given God's Law—the "oracles of God" (see Romans 3:1,2). Yet all of humanity—both Jews and Gentiles—have "the work of the law written in their hearts, their conscience also bearing witness" (Romans 2:15,16). As you go through the Commandments with self-righteous sinners, their consciences bear witness to the truth of the Law.

Anyone who frequently evangelizes the lost will know that self-righteousness is not confined to the Jews. There are millions of *Gentiles* who think that they are good people, and they are quick to boast that they have kept most (if not all) of the Ten Commandments. These folks need the Law to bring them the knowledge of sin.

The Reasonableness of Hell

The fact that Jesus used the Law and made continual reference to future punishment cannot be denied. In light of this, why does the Church today so often avoid talking about sin, righteousness, and judgment? We seem to have removed from the gospel proclamation anything that makes a sinner feel uncomfortable or guilty. But the reality is that sinners *are* guilty, and unless we help them understand that, they will end up in hell.

I believe one major reason that the Church leans toward this kind of gentle, "seeker-friendly" evangelism is that it has left the Law of God out of the equation. Talking about hell and Judgment Day *is* likely to offend sinners—*as long as they don't think they deserve to go there*. Their attitude is understandable. This is a very important point.

An unbeliever will conveniently draw on a belief in hell if someone rapes and strangles his beloved daughter. He will grit his teeth and say, "I hope that man rots in hell!" As far as the world is concerned, hell is only for extremely evil people who torture and murder other human beings. It is not a place for good-hearted humanity.

But when we go through the Ten Commandments to show a man his sin, he will understand that he has violated the moral Law of a holy and just God, and hell then becomes *reasonable* to him. Using the moral Law in conjunction with future punishment will make the gospel make sense. It's what Jesus did—and we must follow His example.

Jonathan Edwards says,

> By a clear discovery of the connection between their sin and God's wrath, they are sensible of their danger of hell, of which many are in a measure sensible, who are wholly insensible of their desert of hell. The threatenings of the law make them afraid indeed, that God will punish sins.

If we preach a message that doesn't offend and cut deep into the conscience, we may fill our churches with people who don't understand that they have sinned against the Lord.

Think of how the prophet Nathan approached King David after he had committed adultery and murder. Consider the *personal* and condemnatory nature of the rebuke. By modern standards, it seems that Nathan was deliberately insensitive to David. There was nothing gentle about his words. He said that the king had *despised* the commandment of the Lord, that he had done *evil* in the sight of God. David had committed murder and adultery, and the prophet boldly pronounced stinging judgment upon the king.

But look at the wonderful result of Nathan's faithfulness to God: "David said to Nathan, 'I have sinned against the LORD'" (2 Samuel 12:13). If we preach a message that doesn't offend and cut deep into the conscience, we may fill our churches, but they will be filled with people who don't understand that they have *sinned against the Lord*, and if there's no repentance, there is no salvation.

Jesus and Zacchaeus

It is easy to read the account of Zacchaeus and conclude that mere inquisitiveness brought him to salvation. He ran ahead of Jesus, climbed a tree, and was duly called down by the Savior. However, the Bible makes it clear that it takes more than curiosity to bring a sinner to a saving knowledge of Jesus Christ. We must *strive* to enter the narrow gate (see Luke 13:24). The Greek word for "strive" is derived from the word "agonize." Since Scripture says that there are *none* who seek after God (see Romans 3:11), if anyone comes to Christ, it is because the merciful hand of the Father draws him to the Savior (see John 6:44).

For Zacchaeus to be saved, he had to have an understanding that he had sinned against God and therefore needed a Savior. The Scriptures also tell us that he was a Jew (see Luke 19:9) who knew the Law (revealed in verse 8; see Exodus 22:1; 2 Samuel 12:6).

The fact that he *climbed up a tree* to see Jesus revealed that he was more than curious. Obviously, his lack of stature was the reason for the tree climbing, but his actions also reveal that he had a humble heart. No doubt there weren't many proud Pharisees climbing trees to see Jesus.

It is therefore very likely that Zacchaeus had a knowledge of sin via the Law, and that awareness made him *desperate* for grace. It caused him to thirst for righteousness and humbly seek after the Savior.

Jesus and Nicodemus

Nicodemus had more than the work of the Law written on his heart; he also had the Law written in stone by the finger of God—the Ten Commandments. He had the *advantage* of being a Jew (see Romans 3:1,2). The Jews had been given the moral Law, and that was a great benefit. He was obviously well versed in the Law because the Bible tells us that he was a "ruler of the Jews" and a "teacher in Israel" (see John 3:2–10). John Bunyan says of the necessity of knowing the Law:

> The man who does not know the nature of the Law, cannot know the nature of sin.

Nicodemus came to Jesus in the darkness of the night, seeking the light of the truth. He humbly acknowledged the deity of the Son of God, saying, "We know that You are a teacher come from God; for no one can do these signs that You do unless God is with him" (verse 2).

Preceding the discourse between Nicodemus and Jesus, the Bible tells us that Jesus knew all men, and that He "had no need that anyone should testify of man, for He knew what was in man" (John 2:24,25). Jesus knew that Nicodemus was a man of humble heart, so He gave him the message of grace.

Again, we see the principle of grace being given to the humble. If a man is thirsting for righteousness, he shouldn't be given the thirst-creating salt of the Law, but the quenching waters of the gospel of grace (John 3:15–17).

Jesus and Nathanael

The account of Nathanael coming to the Savior baffled me for years. He was sitting under a tree when Philip sought him out and told him that he had found the Messiah. Despite Nathanael's prejudice toward those who lived in Nazareth, he followed Philip and embraced the Savior, simply because Jesus said that He saw him sitting under the tree. It would seem that the salvation of a soul is simple. But there is more here than first meets the eye.

Here are the missing puzzle pieces. In John 1:47, Jesus tells us that Nathanael was an "Israelite" who was therefore brought up under the Law. He was an Israelite "indeed" (not just in word; he didn't twist the Law and make its power void), and he had "no guile." In other words, he lacked any deceit. Here was another humble, godly Jew who was seeking the truth.

Without an understanding of the function of the Law, one could easily fall into the trap of thinking that people can come to the Savior without any depth of the knowledge of sin. It is no wonder that so many Christians think the salvation of a soul is simply a matter of praying a simple prayer—just find a sinner under a tree (or up a tree) and bring him to Jesus. But millions have already made a Lawless profession of faith under the hand of modern methods. It seems that they have entered through the door of salvation without a knowledge of sin. Again, consider the warning of Jesus: "*Strive* to enter through the narrow gate, for many, I say to you, will seek to enter and will not be able" (Luke 13:24, emphasis added). The terrible truth is that these misguided sinners have entered another door—the door of false conversion.[34] That door may be a way that seems right to a man, but it is a door that doesn't provide entrance into heaven.

No doubt the Law had done its usual preparatory work on the heart of Nathanael, and perhaps under that tree he was crying out to God for salvation. More than likely he was laboring and heavy laden under the weight of his personal sin, and the Law acted its part as a schoolmaster to bring him to Christ, where he found rest for his soul (see Matthew 11:29).

Jesus and the Woman at the Well

Jesus often spoke to vast crowds, but He also went out of His way to speak to individuals when they were alone. Experience shows that people tend to be more open when they aren't subject to the peer pressure of friends.

---

[34] For further teaching on this sobering subject, see *The Way of the Master* by Ray Comfort and Kirk Cameron (Tyndale House Publishers).

We are told that Jesus "needed" to go through Samaria (John 4:4), implying that He had a divine encounter with one woman. Here Jesus uses the essence of the Seventh Commandment to bring conviction to this adulterous woman:

> Jesus said to her, "Go, call your husband, and come here." The woman answered and said, "I have no husband." Jesus said to her, "You have well said, 'I have no husband,' for you have had five husbands, and the one whom you now have is not your husband; in that you spoke truly." (John 4:16–18)

Like many people today, she had had multiple husbands (verse 18), and was now shacked up with another man. She was therefore transgressing the Seventh Commandment:

> So then if, while her husband lives, she marries another man, she will be called an adulteress; but if her husband dies, she is free from that law,[35] so that she is no adulteress, though she has married another man. (Romans 7:3)

This woman was clearly violating the Law, and Jesus confronted her on the issue to help her see her sin.

Relationship Evangelism

Saint Francis of Assisi once said, "Preach the gospel. Where necessary, use words." Perhaps his meaning was, "Don't just preach mere words. Let this sinful world also see the reality

---

[35] God's Law, not man's.

of your faith by your good works." However, many within the Church have latched onto this saying to justify "lifestyle evangelism." According to a recent Barna Group survey, 74 percent of born-again adults engage in this method of sharing their faith, which is "living in ways that would impress non-Christians and cause them to raise questions about that lifestyle."[36]

Another popular method is called "relationship evangelism," in which Christians build a relationship with a sinner, and over time earn the right to talk to him about the salvation of his soul. This could take days, weeks, months, or even years. But ask yourself, who are the hardest people to reach with the gospel? Isn't it our unsaved loved ones—our family members and friends? We don't want to offend loved ones because it could damage the relationship. The same is true with our neighbors and coworkers. So why then would we want to build relationships with people we want to witness to? That would only make witnessing to them more difficult because if we offend them, we risk losing the relationships that we've built.

In reality, it is far easier to talk to strangers about their salvation, because we can be open and honest and talk about sin, righteousness, and judgment.

---

[36] Barna Group, "Survey Shows How Christians Share Their Faith," January 31, 2005 <www.barna.org>.

In reality, it is far easier to talk to strangers about their salvation, because we can be open and honest and talk about sin, righteousness, and judgment. If our openness offends them and they walk away, we haven't lost a relationship, because a meaningful one hasn't been established. And our effort to talk with them about spiritual matters shows that, even as strangers, we care about them and are concerned about their eternal destiny.

How long did Jesus take to build a relationship with the woman at the well before He spoke to her about her sin? It seems that it was just a few minutes. How long did He build a relationship with Zacchaeus before He called him down from the tree and spoke of spiritual things? The truth is, none of us can afford to wait very long, because the sinner may die—and end up in the Lake of Fire—while we are busy trying to build a rapport with him. The Scriptures tell us that *now* is the accepted time; *today* is the day of salvation (see 2 Corinthians 6:2).

Jesus and Saul of Tarsus

It is easy to be overawed by Saul's Road to Damascus experience. Here was a man so zealous for God that he was hunting Christians like a hungry bloodhound. He thought that by sniffing them out, and then snuffing them out, he was doing God a great service.

As Saul was traveling to Damascus, a brilliant light shone from heaven and Jesus spoke directly to him. The experience stopped him dead in his tracks, but in the Book of

Romans we see once again that there is more to this than meets the eye. Consider what influenced his conversion prior to this dramatic incident:

> What shall we say then? Is the law sin? Certainly not! On the contrary, I would not have known sin except through the law. For I would not have known covetousness unless the law had said, "You shall not covet."[37]
>
> But sin, taking opportunity by the commandment, produced in me all manner of evil desire. For apart from the law sin was dead. I was alive once without the law, but when the commandment came, sin revived and I died. And the commandment, which was to bring life, I found to bring death. For sin, taking occasion by the commandment, deceived me, and by it killed me. Therefore the law is holy, and the commandment holy and just and good.
>
> Has then what is good become death to me? Certainly not! But sin, that it might appear sin, was producing death in me through what is good, so that sin through the commandment might become exceedingly sinful. (Romans 7:7–13)

It was the Law that showed him what sin was. Paul not only recognized his personal transgression of the Tenth Commandment (verse 7), but he also admitted his trans-

---

[37] Tenth Commandment.

gression of the Third Commandment, saying, "I was formerly a blasphemer..." (1 Timothy 1:13).

However, some insist that when Paul referred to "the law" in Romans 7, he was speaking about the entire Old Testament, rather than the Ten Commandments. But look once more at his wording—he actually *quotes* the Tenth Commandment (verse 7). Why would he do that if he were simply referring to the Old Testament in general, and not specifically the Ten Commandments? And why would he call the Old Testament "the commandment"?

Martin Luther writes in reference to this passage,

> "I was alive without the law once: but when the commandment came, sin revived" (Romans 7:9). So it is with the work-righteous and the proud unbelievers. Because they do not know the Law of God, which is directed against them, it is impossible for them to know their sin. Therefore also they are not amenable to instruction. If they would know the Law, they would also know their sin; and sin to which they are now dead would become alive in them.

The Law shows us *specifically* what we have done wrong and reveals our need for the Savior. The light of His creation, the light of conscience, and societal standards are not enough to awaken us to our true state before God. Remember Luther's words—failure to use the Law will leave a sinner "not amenable to instruction." Why do men spurn the gospel? For the same reason that a man, thinking he is safe as he sits on an airplane, will spurn a parachute that is offered to him. If he is suddenly convinced that he has to jump 25,000 feet, then he becomes amenable to instruction on how to put on and open the parachute in which he had no interest moments before.

The Law was clearly evident in leading to Paul's conversion. The Law didn't save him. It brought him to the risen Savior, who saved him. The Law showed him that he needed to be delivered from the power of sin, or sin would deliver him to death and hell. It's true that salvation came to Saul out of the blue, but the knowledge that he needed the Savior came to him out of the blackness of Mount Sinai.

All of humanity needs a Road to Damascus experience. People must be turned back from the dark Road to Damnation through the light of a personal encounter with Jesus of Nazareth. Like Saul of Tarsus, they must be kept under guard by the Law (see Galatians 3:23) before they enter the kingdom of God through the Door of the Savior.

What We Have Here is a Failure to... Believe?

It's understandable why so many don't use the Law to reach the lost. Again, I didn't see its use in evangelism for the first ten years of my Christian walk. Since then, I have heard many grateful Christians say, "Why didn't I see this before? It is so obvious!" The reason we don't see it is that we are blind to it. For example, consider the following argument against this principle.

Some have claimed that the disciples did not deem it necessary to deliver the "bad news" ("the Law condemns you") as a necessary prologue to the "good news about Jesus." Instead, they argue, the very heart of the message the disciples proclaimed was that "by Him everyone who believes is justified from all things from which you could not be justified by the law of Moses" (Acts 13:39).

However, the very text cited is an example of the Law bringing the bad news before the good news. The inspired record explains that the bad news is that the Law of Moses cannot justify you. That prepares the heart for the good news that through Jesus we can be justified. That's exactly what we should tell both Jews and Gentiles. We need to say that their attempts to keep the Commandments cannot make them right with God ("the Law cannot save you"), but that God Himself has provided another way ("the gospel of the grace of God"). That is the principle of "Law before grace."

Another common argument is that repentance is required, not because of our *guilt under the Law*, but because of *unbelief* in the One whom God had sent, as stated in John 16:8–11. So let's look closely at these verses, and see if we need to repent because of the sin of not believing in Jesus:

> "And when He has come, He will convict the world of sin, and of righteousness, and of judgment: of sin, because they do not believe in Me ..." (John 16:8,9)

At face value, it seems Jesus is saying that the world will be judged for their sin "because they do not believe in Me." That would mean that sin is "a failure to believe in Jesus."

Let's say you are a missionary in the heart of Africa, and you find a tribe of people who don't speak English. They can't read. They have never heard of the Bible or of Jesus Christ. They, like the Athenians of Acts 17, are ignorant of the truth. You have been commanded to imitate Paul, so your message will be the same as his to the Athenians—that

A great deal of damage has been done to the cause of the gospel by Christians who tell the lost that they will go to hell "because they don't believe in Jesus."

"God...commands all men everywhere to repent, because He has appointed a day on which He will judge the world in righteousness" (verses 30,31). You know that without the Savior the tribespeople will end up in hell for eternity. Why? Because they have sinned against God. What is their sin? According to this thinking, it is that they have *failed* to believe in Jesus.

That creates a big problem for you. The dilemma is that they haven't yet *failed* to believe in Jesus *because they have never heard of Him.* As Paul said, "How shall they believe in Him of whom they have not heard?" (Romans 10:14). If that is the case, they haven't yet sinned. According to that logic, Romans 3:23 is clearly wrong. It says that *all* have sinned— yet here is a tribe that has no sin. Of course, Scripture is not wrong, so the meaning of the passage in John 16 is obviously deeper than what it appears.

A great deal of damage has been done to the cause of the gospel by well-meaning Christians who tell the lost that they will go to hell "because they don't believe in Jesus." Understandably, this makes no sense to them. They recognize that it's unreasonable for God to eternally damn them just for not believing something. However, the passage in John 16 can be explained this way:

If a man jumps out of a plane without a parachute, he will perish because he transgressed the law of gravity. Had he put on a parachute, he would have been saved. In one sense, it's true that he perished because he didn't put on the parachute. But the *primary* reason he died was because he broke the law of gravity.

If a sinner refuses to trust in Jesus Christ when he passes through the door of death, he will perish. This isn't because he failed to believe in the Savior, but *primarily* because he transgressed the Law of God. Had he "put on the Lord Jesus Christ" (Romans 13:14), he would have been saved; but because he refused to repent, he will suffer the full consequences of his sin. Again, sin is not "failing to believe in Jesus." The Bible tells us, "Sin is transgression of the law" (1 John 3:4, KJV).

If we find ourselves preaching to a tribe in the heart of Africa, we would do well to follow Paul's example in Acts chapter 17, and preach the essence of the First and Second

Commandments. He told them that God had overlooked the times of their ignorance, that they were idolaters,[38] and that they needed to therefore put the God who created all things first in their affections.[39] They had failed to do so, and now God commanded them to repent. Then Paul faithfully preached the reality of Judgment Day.

The idea that sin is "failure to believe in Jesus" leads to another difficulty. That God would send anyone to hell just for not believing in Jesus is a difficult pill for *Christians* to swallow. So they often espouse a belief that no one will go to hell without first having a chance to believe in Jesus. This is contrary to Scripture. God is not obligated to give us mercy. He is only obligated by His own righteousness to give us justice. He *must* do what is right and just, and He cannot let evil go unpunished. God "will render to each one according to his deeds" (Romans 2:6). Our punishment is *deserved*; mercy is mercy precisely because it is *undeserved*. Again, He's not obligated to give us mercy, only justice.

That's what makes grace so amazing. And when the Law shows us the depth of our sin, and its just punishment, it fills us with gratitude to God for the incredible mercy we have received through the gospel. John Newton, who wrote "Amazing Grace," clearly understood this. He said, "Ignorance of the nature and design of the Law is at the bottom of most religious mistakes."

[38] Second Commandment.
[39] First Commandment.

Chapter Five

WHAT DID PAUL DO? (PART ONE)

The apostle Paul's greatest passion was for the salvation of the lost. Consider his personal priority: He pleaded, "[Pray] for me, that utterance may be given to me, that I may open my mouth boldly to make known the mystery of the gospel,...that in it I may speak boldly, *as I ought to speak*" (Ephesians 6:19,20, emphasis added).

So, what did Paul do when it came to fulfilling his commission? Time and time again, we see him going into synagogues and preaching the gospel to the unsaved. The Bible tells us the identity of his audience:

Then Paul stood up, and motioning with his hand said, "*Men of Israel, and you who fear God*, listen." (Acts 13:16, emphasis added)

"Men and brethren, *sons of the family of Abraham, and those among you who fear God*, to you the word of this salvation has been sent." (Acts 13:26, emphasis added)

Scripture gives us insight into the condition of the soil on which the seed was being sown. Those who were proud and didn't fear God needed the Law to make them tremble. Those who *did* fear God were trembling, already humbled, and therefore needed to hear the message of grace. So Paul preached the cross. He told them that the Law in which they trusted couldn't justify them; they needed the forgiveness of sins, and only through Jesus could they receive it.

John Wesley comments on Paul's preaching in this passage, pointing out his use of the Law coupled with future punishment:

The very first sermon of St. Paul's which is recorded, concludes in these words: "By him all that believe are justified from all things, from which you could not be justified by the law of Moses. Beware therefore, lest that come upon you which is spoken of in the Prophets; Behold, you despisers, and wonder, and perish: For I work a work in your days, a work which you will in no wise believe, though a man declare it unto you." (Acts 13:39–41)

Now it is manifest, all this is preaching the Law, in the sense wherein you understand the term; even although great part of, if not all, his hearers, were either Jews or religious proselytes, (Verse 43) and, therefore, probably many of them, in some degree at least, convicted of sin already. He first reminds them, that they could not be justified by the Law of Moses, but only by faith in Christ; and then severely threatens them with the judgments of God, which is in the strongest sense, preaching the Law.[40]

After the hardhearted Jews rejected Paul's message, we are told that he would thereafter preach the gospel to the Gentiles:

"It was necessary that the word of God should be spoken to you first; but since you reject it, and judge yourselves unworthy of everlasting life, behold, we turn to the Gentiles." (Acts 13:46)

Wesley then comments on Acts 14:15:

In his next discourse, that to the Heathens at Lystra, (14:15ff.) we do not find so much as the name of Christ: The whole purport of it is, that they should "turn from those vain idols,[41] unto the living God." Now confess the truth. Do not you think, if you had been there, you could have preached much better than

---

[40] John Wesley, "The Law Established Through Faith," Sermon 35 <http://gbgm-umc.org/umhistory/wesley/sermons/serm-035.stm>.

[41] First and Second Commandments.

he? I should not wonder if you thought too, that his preaching so ill occasioned his being so ill-treated; and that his being stoned was a just judgment upon him for not preaching Christ![42]

Wesley says it wouldn't surprise him if preachers of his day thought that Paul's ill treatment was punishment by God for *failing* to preach Christ. There are also those within modern Christendom who consider Paul to be an inadequate preacher, thinking he lacked the "light" given to the contemporary Church. However, it's clear that Paul was ill-treated and stoned by his hearers *because he wasn't seeker-friendly*. Instead, he spoke boldly, "as [he] ought to speak." He knew that his listeners must be humbled by the Law; they must understand that they had sinned against God before they could appreciate the gospel. He therefore told them to turn from idols to God. He was faithful, even if it caused great offense and led to his own death (see Acts 20:22–24).

Paul in Jail

In Acts 16:22–33, we read that Paul and Silas had been beaten and thrown into prison. It must have been an interesting night. They sang and prayed, and no doubt shared the gospel with those around them, since that was the purpose for which Paul lived. He said, "Woe is me if I do not preach the gospel" (1 Corinthians 9:16); he made himself a servant to all men that he might win them for Christ (verse 19).

---

[42] Wesley, ibid.

Paul and Silas were true and faithful witnesses, even while in prison. They had a captive audience. Their verbal testimony seems to be evidenced by the fact that after an earthquake hit the prison, the jailer came trembling to them and asked, "What must I do to be saved?" The ground had stopped shaking, so he was obviously inquiring how to be saved from something more fearful than a mere earthquake. Paul therefore answered him with a simple word about trusting in the Savior.

Fortunately, we don't need to wait for an actual earthquake to have people ask how they can be saved. We can shake them to the very core by using God's Law to make them tremble.

Once again, we must remember that if someone humbly asks, "What must I do to be saved?" we shouldn't give the person the moral Law. Its purpose is to show people that they are guilty sinners and need to be saved from God's wrath. Once they have this knowledge, they no longer need to be made to tremble—they are obviously aware of their need, as their question makes clear. We should therefore give them the message of the grace of God. We should preach the simplicity of the gospel, as Paul did.

A Gaping Hole

How thankful I am to have the writings of John Wesley, whose life proved his heart. His passion was the heartbeat of God, and the very heart of God is to reach the lost. That was what put Jesus on the cross.

Like Paul, Wesley burned with evangelistic zeal, and one can feel his tenacity when it comes to the evangelistic use of the Law. He was like a fisherman who had been issued an official, proven net, and he refused to even consider the use of a cheap net that was filled with holes.

How can any preacher who has a fear of God omit a word like "repentance" from his message? That leaves a gaping hole in the net. The justification often given for leaving the word out of our vocabulary is that the world doesn't understand its meaning. But why should we dumb down our message for our hearers? We should instead educate them by explaining what repentance means. When I mention "repentance" as I'm preaching the gospel open-air to unsaved people, I say, "That's an old-fashioned word that means to 'turn from sin.' It's not enough to just confess your sins to God—you must *forsake* them."

Even the secular media refuses to dumb down their message for their audience. They regularly use words like "unrepentant" to describe a hardened criminal who has no remorse for his crime. They even use biblical words like "contrition" when someone is sorry for what he has done. But not the modern Church.

In the name of sensitivity, many today have diluted the entire bottle of medicine. While watering down the medicine removes the bitter taste and makes it more palatable, it reduces its curative properties. When we leave out any mention of the Law and the personal nature of sin, we leave the conscience dormant. If there's no conviction of sin, there's no repentance from sin. And without repentance, one cannot be saved. The grim result is a graveyard of church members who have never tasted the life regeneration of the Holy Spirit. On the Day that they cry, "Lord, Lord," they will wish beyond measure that preachers had used the words "hell, wrath, repentance, Law, and Lake of Fire," because on that Day they will fully understand their meaning.

We are seeing the fulfillment of the prophecy of William Booth, founder of the Salvation Army. He warned,

> I consider that the chief dangers which will confront the 20th century will be: religion without the Holy Spirit, Christianity without Christ, forgiveness without regeneration, morality without God, and heaven without hell.

Listen as a resolute John Wesley, in a rather lengthy but wonderful quote, speaks to the seeker-friendly folks of his day about Paul's method of preaching:

> To the gaoler [jailer] indeed, when "he sprang in, and came trembling, and fell down before Paul and Silas, and said, Sirs, what must I do to be saved?" he immediately said, "Believe on the Lord Jesus Christ;" (Acts 16:29–31) and in the case of one so deeply convicted of sin, who would not have said the same? But to the men of Athens you find him speaking in a quite different manner; reproving their superstition, ignorance, and idolatry; and strongly moving them to repent, from the consideration of a future judgment, and of the resur-

rection from the dead (Acts 17:24–31). Likewise when Felix sent for Paul, on purpose that he might "hear him concerning the faith in Christ;" instead of preaching Christ in *your* sense, (which would probably have caused the Governor either to mock or to contradict and blaspheme) "he reasoned of righteousness, temperance, and judgment to come," till Felix (hardened as he was) "trembled." (24:24, 25) Go thou, and tread in his steps. Preach Christ to the careless sinner, by reasoning "of righteousness, temperance, and judgment to come!"

If you say, "But he preached Christ in a different manner in his Epistles:" I answer,

(1.) He did not there preach at all; not in that sense wherein we speak: For preaching, in our present question, means speaking before a congregation. But, waving this, I answer,

(2.) His Epistles are directed, not to unbelievers, such as those we are now speaking of, but "to the saints of God," in Rome, Corinth, Philippi, and other places. Now, unquestionably, he would speak more of Christ to these than to those who were without God in the world. And yet,

(3.) Every one of these is full of the Law, even the Epistles to the Romans and the Galatians; in both of which he does what you term "preaching the Law," and that to believers, as well as unbelievers.

From hence it is plain, you know not what it is to preach Christ, in the sense of the Apostle. For doubtless St. Paul judged himself to be preaching Christ, both to Felix, and at Antioch, Lystra, and Athens: From whose example every thinking man must infer, that not only the declaring the love of Christ to sinners, but also the declaring that He will come from heaven in flaming fire, is, in the Apostle's sense, preaching Christ; yea, in the full scriptural meaning of the word. To preach Christ, is to preach what He hath revealed, either in the Old or New Testament; so that you are really preaching Christ, when you are saying, "The wicked shall be turned into hell, and all the people that forget God," as when you are saying, "Behold the Lamb of God, which taketh away the sin of the world!"

Consider this well—that to preach Christ, is to preach all things that Christ hath spoken; all his promises; all his threatenings and commands; all that is written in his book; and then you will know how to preach Christ, without making void the Law.

Paul, who zealously desired to reach the lost, did not dilute his message. He faithfully preached about sin, called men to repent, and warned of future punishment.

Paul in Athens

Paul's spirit was stirred when he saw the idolatry of the Athenians. Every Christian should be stirred to action by the sin of idolatry because it is an easy pathway to hell. A transgression of the Second Commandment, idolatry is a tantalizing and tasty morsel to feed the sinful human heart.

If sinners have an idolatrous concept of God as a benign philanthropic figure, with no reference to sin, righteousness, or judgment, then there is no need for them to have any concern about their sinful condition.

So each day, Paul shared his faith with the Jews and devout (godly) people (see Acts 17:17), and then he preached open-air.[43] He told them that God was not an idol, that He made all things, and that He was omnipresent (verses 22–28). He again preached the essence of the First and Second Commandments. What better way is there to tell sinners that God should be the focal point of their affections than to say that they should have no other gods before Him? What better way is there to expose idolatry than to say that God Himself said (in the Second Commandment) that we should make no "graven image"? Look at Paul's words:

> "Therefore, since we are the offspring of God, we ought not to think that the Divine Nature is like gold or silver or stone, something shaped by art and man's devising. Truly, these times of ignorance God overlooked, but now commands all men everywhere to repent, because He has appointed a day on which He will judge the world in righteousness..." (Acts 17:29–31)

---

[43] For an in-depth at the subject of open-air preaching, see *The World's Greatest Preachers* by Kirk Cameron and Ray Comfort (Whitaker House). We also have videos that show open-air preaching in action. See www.livingwaters.com.

Paul told his hearers that the God of Israel was their Creator. He overlooked their ignorance of the past, but now He commanded them to repent. Paul preached the essence of the Law, then repentance and future punishment.

By preaching repentance, he wasn't merely telling them to change their minds about God and sin. He was telling the prodigals to get up out of the pigsty *and leave it*. They were to *turn from sin* to the God they had offended. The reason they were commanded to repent was because God had "appointed a day on which He will judge the world in righteousness." That "righteousness" is the perfect righteousness that is of the perfect Law (see Psalm 19:7; Romans 2:12; James 2:12), given by a perfect God who demands perfection. The cited verses make it clear that God's standards haven't change since Sinai. Sinners then needed to be saved from the wrath of God's Law, and the same applies right up until Judgment Day. The justice of Almighty God will be enforced on that terrible Day: "He shall judge the world in righteousness, and He shall administer judgment for the peoples in uprightness" (Psalm 9:8).

Paul in Ephesus

When Peter preached to the *humble* Jews on the Day of Pentecost, they were "cut to the heart" and asked, "What shall we do?" (Acts 2:37). They were repentant. But when he preached to *proud* Jews they were "furious and plotted to kill them" (Acts 5:33). When Stephen told proud Jews that they had violated God's Law (see Acts 7:54), they were also "cut to the heart, and they gnashed at him with their teeth." It seems that the mere mention that they had transgressed the Law brought conviction of sin to their proud hearts.

The apostle Paul also caused "a great commotion" when he preached (see Acts 19:23). He wasn't generally a popular preacher, based on how the crowds reacted to his words:

- Acts 13:45: The crowd began "contradicting and blaspheming."

- Acts 13:50: Paul and Barnabas were persecuted and thrown out of the region.

- Acts 14:5: The crowd plotted to stone them, forcing them to flee.

- Acts 14:19: Paul was stoned and left for dead.

- Acts 16:23: Both Paul and Silas were beaten with "many stripes" and thrown in prison.

- Acts 18:6: Paul's hearers "opposed him and blasphemed."

- Acts 19:28: His hearers were "full of wrath" and seized Paul's companions.

- Acts 20:23: The Holy Spirit warned Paul that chains and tribulations awaited him wherever he preached the gospel.

- Acts 22:22: His listeners called for his death.

- Acts 23:1,2: As soon as Paul began to speak, he was smacked in the mouth.

- Acts 23:10. After Paul spoke, there was "great dissension" in the crowd and he was nearly "pulled to pieces."

- Acts 23:12,13: More than forty Jews conspired to murder him.

- Acts 24:5: He is called a "plague," a "creator of dissension," and a "ringleader" of a "sect."

Why was there such an uproar about his message? Because of its uncompromising content. Listen to what his hearers said of its substance:

> "Moreover you see and hear that not only at Ephesus, but throughout almost all Asia, this Paul has persuaded and turned away many people, *saying that they are not gods which are made with hands.*" (Acts 19:26, emphasis added)

These people were idolaters, so it makes sense that he preached the heart of the First and Second Commandments, as he did in Athens. Some maintain that he simply preached the gospel, but saying that there are no gods made with human hands is more than a message of "Christ crucified." It is clear that Paul preached the fundamental nature of God's Law, in order to bring his hearers to the knowledge of sin and true repentance.

When Paul left the elders of Ephesus, he said that he was "testifying to Jews, and also to Greeks, repentance toward God and faith toward our Lord Jesus Christ" (Acts 20:21). Those who preach that repentance is merely a change of mind about God need to change their minds themselves about what God says on this issue. The Bible declares, "Let everyone who names the name of Christ *depart* from iniquity [lawlessness]" (2 Timothy 2:19, emphasis added).

If sinners are told to merely name the name of Christ (to change their mind about Him), and they therefore fail to *depart* from iniquity, they will end up in that great multitude who will cry out to Jesus on the Day of Judgment and hear the horrifying words, "Depart from Me, you who practice lawlessness" (Matthew 7:21–23). Those who refuse to depart from lawlessness will be commanded to depart from the Lord. We cannot serve both sin and the Savior. To "repent" means to *confess* and *forsake* sin:

> He who covers his sins will not prosper, but whoever confesses and *forsakes* them will have mercy. (Proverbs 28:13, emphasis added)

Obviously, we are not saved *by* repentance. We are saved by grace, through faith in Christ alone, and repentance is the outworking of saving faith. While it is correct to say that New Testament repentance speaks of an inner change of attitude and heart, this results in a change of conduct. The root of grace produces the fruit of repentance.

God is deeply affronted by sin—the cross provides ample evidence of that fact. But because many within the Church today have disregarded the moral Law, they think lightly of sin and so they believe repentance is merely a change of mind about God. However, when sin is seen in the light of the Law (that it is "*exceedingly* sinful"), it can be understood why we must *forsake* that which is an offense to God.

Jonathan Edwards states,

> The only way we can know whether we are sinning is by knowing His moral Law.

Paul yearned to see true conversion among his listeners. He wanted them to experience genuine repentance, and to enable sinners to understand what they must repent of, he had to preach the Law. For Paul to do so would have been an outworking of his own teaching. He practiced what he preached.

Paul and the Colossians

In addressing the Colossians, the apostle explains why God's wrath will come upon the children of disobedience:

> Therefore put to death your members which are on the earth: fornication,[44] uncleanness, passion, evil desire, and covetousness,[45] which is idolatry.[46] Because

---

[44] Seventh Commandment.
[45] Tenth Commandment.
[46] Second Commandment.

of these things the wrath of God[47] is coming upon the sons of disobedience, in which you yourselves once walked when you lived in them. But now you yourselves are to put off all these: anger, wrath,[48] malice, blasphemy,[49] filthy language out of your mouth. Do not lie[50] to one another, since you have put off the old man with his deeds... (Colossians 3:5–9)

Here Paul lists six of the Ten Commandments and relates them to the coming wrath of God for those who disobey.

Paul in Thessalonica

When he evangelized the Thessalonians, Paul didn't confine his preaching to the good news of the gospel:

For they themselves declare concerning us what manner of entry we had to you, and how you turned to God from idols[51] to serve the living and true God and to wait for His Son from heaven, whom He raised from the dead, even Jesus who delivers us from the wrath to come. (1 Thessalonians 1:9,10)

When Paul came to them, they turned to God from idols. Obviously, this was because they were informed that idolatry (transgression of the Second Commandment) was

---

[47] Future punishment.
[48] Sixth Commandment.
[49] Third Commandment.
[50] Ninth Commandment.
[51] Second Commandment.

sin in the sight of the only true God. Again, he didn't neglect to speak of the wrath to come.

First Thessalonians chapter 2 gives us insight into Paul's ministry and the attitude and motives of those who preached with him:

- He had faith that his labor wasn't in vain (verse 1).

- Even though Paul and his companions were spitefully treated, they were bold in the face of much opposition (verse 2).

- Their motive for preaching was pure (verse 3).

- They saw their preaching as a great privilege (verse 4).

- They had a direct responsibility toward God Himself (verse 4).

- They refused to use flattering words in their preaching (verse 5).

- They didn't preach for monetary gain (verse 5).

- They did not seek the praise of men (verse 6).

- They were moved by gentleness (verse 7).

- Love was their inspiration (verse 8).

- They were totally committed to reaching others with the gospel (verse 9).

- They were blameless (verse 10).

Like Jesus, Paul's agenda wasn't to be "sensitive" to sinners. He was sensitive to the Holy Spirit, not the approval of his hearers. He wanted to clear the temple of sin, so he used the whip of the Law and then, like Jesus, he preached future punishment:

> And to give you who are troubled rest with us when the Lord Jesus is revealed from heaven with His mighty angels, in flaming fire taking vengeance on those who do not know God, and on those who do not obey the gospel of our Lord Jesus Christ. These shall be punished with everlasting destruction from the presence of the Lord and from the glory of his power... (2 Thessalonians 1:7–9)

This is what Paul believed, and it was therefore what he spoke. He said, "Knowing, therefore, the terror of the Lord, we persuade men" (2 Corinthians 5:11). Charles Spurgeon rightly said, "Some have used the terrors of the Lord to terrify, but Paul used them to persuade." How can we best persuade men that God is to be feared and that they must come to the Savior? Not by leaving fearful words out of our preaching. Removing the mention of wrath, sin, hell, judgment, righteousness, Law, etc., from our message has the opposite effect.

In late November 2004, immediately after President George W. Bush was reelected, ABC News ran a story about the Christian vote. They said that some Christians believed the President owed them moral legislation in payment for his victory. Dr. D. James Kennedy, pastor of Coral Ridge Presbyterian Church in Fort Lauderdale, Florida, was asked, "What would you say to people in those states that are really concerned about the impact that Christian conservatives are going to have on our government?" Kennedy didn't hesitate for a moment. He said, "'Repent! Repent,' that's what I would say."

The interviewer, obviously taken aback by his answer, gave him a second chance to back down a little. After all, this is the day of political correctness, a day in which much of the Church is very careful about offending its hearers. He no doubt thought Kennedy should have been sensitive to all the viewers who might be offended. The interviewer said, "There are millions of people in this country who either are not Christian, or are not Christian in the way in which you are. And when you answer by saying 'Repent,' they may find that either scary or offensive." Kennedy smiled and answered, "I couldn't care less." God bless him.

Paul with Felix

When Paul was brought before the governor, he had a wonderful opportunity to "preach Christ." But again he didn't confine his message to the good news of the gospel:

> Now as he reasoned about righteousness, self-control, and the judgment to come, Felix was afraid and answered, "Go away for now; when I have a convenient time I will call for you." (Acts 24:25)

Scripture records that Felix was afraid. He became fearful, because Paul *reasoned* with him about future punishment. There was judgment to come, and God's standard of righteousness, revealed in the Law, made him fearful. John Wesley's writes concerning this passage:

> When Felix sent for Paul, on purpose that he might "hear him concerning the faith in Christ;" instead of preaching Christ in *your* sense (which would probably have caused the Governor either to mock or to contradict and blaspheme,) "he reasoned of righteousness, temperance, and judgment to come," till Felix (hardened as he was) "trembled" (Acts 24:24,25). Go thou and tread in his steps. Preach Christ to the careless sinner, by reasoning "of righteousness, temperance, and judgment to come!"

Again, why didn't Paul simply tell Felix the good news of the gospel? How would that awaken Felix to his horrifying plight—that he's a guilty sinner headed for hell? The gospel speaks peace; the Law works wrath. It is the Law that shows us that we are at war with God—that we are enemies of God in our minds through wicked works (see Colossians 1:21). Psalm 139:20 confirms this: "Your enemies take Your name in vain."[52] What greater proof can there be that humanity is an enemy of God than to take His holy name in vain, using it as a cuss word to express disgust?

---

[52] Third Commandment.

The Law shows the sinner why God's wrath "abides" on him (see John 3:36). It rouses him to his danger. It makes him quake. Charles Spurgeon warns of those who fail to use the Law to awaken the sinner to his plight:

> Lower the Law and you dim the light by which man perceives his guilt; this is a very serious loss to the sinner rather than a gain; for it lessens the likelihood of his conviction and conversion. I say you have deprived the gospel of its ablest auxiliary [its most powerful weapon] when you have set aside the Law. You have taken away from it the schoolmaster that is to bring men to Christ...They will never accept grace till they tremble before a just and holy Law. Therefore the Law serves a most necessary purpose, and it must not be removed from its place.

From Morning Until Evening

The Scriptures give us further insight into Paul's reasoning as he sought to persuade sinners "concerning Jesus":

> When they had appointed him a day, many came to him at his lodging, to whom he explained and solemnly testified of the kingdom of God, persuading them concerning Jesus from both the Law of Moses and the Prophets, from morning till evening. (Acts 28:23)

Look closely at the content of Paul's preaching. He used both prophecy and the Law of Moses. Prophecy appeals to a man's intellect and creates faith in the Word of God. However, it doesn't bring an awareness of sin. So Paul also persuaded them concerning Jesus from "the Law of Moses." The Law appeals to a man's conscience and brings the knowledge of sin.

Note that Paul *solemnly* testified. The solemn use of the Law was second nature to Paul. He was brought up at the feet of Gamaliel, the great teacher of the Law, and was "taught according to the strictness of our fathers' law..." (Acts 22:3). He knew the Law, and he regularly used it to humble those who transgressed its holy precepts (see Acts 23:3).

By using the Law, Paul was pulling back the veil of Moses so that his hearers could have "the light of the knowledge of the glory of God in the face of Jesus Christ" (2 Corinthians 4:6). William Tyndale said, "Expound the Law truly and open the veil of Moses to condemn all flesh and prove all men sinners, and set at broach the mercy of our Lord Jesus, and let the wounded consciences drink of Him."

In the next chapter we will continue to explore Paul's use of the Law, by opening up the incredible riches of the Book of Romans.

Chapter Six

WHAT DID PAUL DO?
(PART TWO)

In the Book of Romans, Paul not only gives a powerful treatise on the function of the Law, but he uses the Law to bring the knowledge of sin to his readers. He first speaks of future punishment:

> And do you think this, O man, you who judge those practicing such things, and doing the same, that you will escape the judgment of God? (Romans 2:3)

Paul then points out a very important ally that God has given us as we speak to the lost. Scripture tells us that people are rebellious, sin-loving creatures with desperately wicked hearts. The carnal mind hates God's Law and will not subject itself to it (see Romans 8:7). Despite the enmity that humanity has toward the moral Law, we are told that the "work of the law [is] written in their hearts, their conscience also bearing witness" (see Romans 2:15). The *outworking* of God's Law echoes the thundering of Mount Sinai. Its lightning flashes its radiance in the darkness of our ignorance and gives light to every man. The word "conscience" means "with knowledge." We have all been born with the knowledge of right and wrong, so as we speak to the lost about the Law, there is a witness in their hearts telling them that it's true.

The word "conscience" means "with knowledge." We have all been born with the knowledge of right and wrong.

Imagine that a twenty-year-old man is found guilty of rape and murder. His defense counsel maintains that the man had been isolated since birth from all human interaction. No one took the time to teach him right from wrong. Not a soul. He had no moral instruction. Zip. In passing sentence, is the judge going to say, "You viciously raped a woman and strangled her to death, but I am aware that you were never taught right from wrong. I will therefore dismiss your case and declare you not guilty of this crime"? No good judge could ever say that. The guilty man is without excuse because every human being has been *born* with a conscience. It is not something we learn, as some would maintain. While it is *shaped* by our upbringing, it is innate and was given to us along with the gift of our eyes, our ears, and our brain. Regardless of any guidance we have received about right and wrong from our parents and society, none of us can plead moral ignorance as a defense when we stand before God.

A Bed of Sharp Nails

Before opening up the Commandments, Paul rebukes the Jews who "rested" in the Law. No one should *rest* in the Law. That isn't its God-given purpose. It is a bed of sharp nails, whose function is to awaken us from the stupor of deception and get us up out of the bed of self-righteousness:

> Indeed you are called a Jew, and rest on the law, and make your boast in God, and know His will, and approve the things that are excellent, being instructed out of the law. (Romans 2:17,18)

Again, some people question what Paul was referring to when he said "the Law." In the following verses of the same chapter, he makes it clear by referencing four of the Ten Commandments and calling them "the Law":

> You, therefore, who teach another, do you not teach yourself? You who preach that a man should not steal,[53] do you steal? You who say, "Do not commit adultery,"[54] do you commit adultery? You who abhor

---

[53] Eighth Commandment.
[54] Seventh Commandment.

idols,[55] do you rob temples? You who make your boast in the law, do you dishonor God through breaking the law? For "the name of God is blasphemed[56] among the Gentiles because of you," as it is written. (Romans 2:21–24)

Remember, it was the Law that prepared Paul's own heart for the grace of the gospel. He preached the Law, not only because Scripture says it is perfect and converts the soul (Psalm 19:7), but because he knew experientially of its incredible power.

The Law brings the knowledge of sin, stops the mouth of self-justification, and leaves the whole world guilty before God.

In the passage cited above, notice what Paul does with the Commandments. He quotes them, then he applies them personally to his listeners by asking if they had stolen, committed adultery, or been guilty of idolatry.

I have learned to present the gospel in the same way. I ask the individual if he thinks he is a good person. Most people do, as Proverbs 20:6 tells us: "Most men will proclaim each his own goodness." If he says that he is, I simply ask, "Have you ever told a lie? Have you ever stolen something?" As we go through the Law, it brings the knowledge of sin and his conscience bears witness of his guilt. This is not a "cookie cutter" approach, or a method I in-

55 Second Commandment.
56 Third Commandment.

vented. It is based in Scripture. We will look further into how to do this in Chapter 12.

After explaining that Jews and Greeks alike are all under sin (Romans 3:9), Paul reiterates the function of the Law:

> Now we know that whatever the law says, it says to those who are under the law, that every mouth may be stopped, and all the world may become guilty before God. Therefore by the deeds of the law no flesh will be justified in His sight, for by the law is the knowledge of sin. (Romans 3:19,20)

The Law brings the knowledge of sin, stops the mouth of self-justification, and leaves the whole world guilty before God. As Paul preached to the unsaved, how could he bring the knowledge of sin and leave his hearers guilty before God, without using the Law?

Consider how *The Amplified Bible* describes the meaning of Romans 3:20:

> For no person will be justified (made righteous, acquitted, and judged acceptable) in His sight by observing the works prescribed by the Law. For [the real function of] the Law is to make men[57] recognize and be conscious of sin [not mere perception, but an acquaintance with sin which works towards repentance, faith, and holy character].

---

[57] Note that this refers to all "men," and not just Jews.

In Romans 13:8,9, Paul again refers to "the Law," then clarifies what he means by "Law" by naming five of the Ten Commandments:

> Owe no one anything except to love one another, for he who loves another has fulfilled the law. For the commandment, "You shall not commit adultery,"[58] "You shall not murder,"[59] "You shall not steal,"[60] "You shall not bear false witness,"[61] "You shall not covet,"[62] and if there is any other commandment, are all summed up in this saying, namely, "You shall love your neighbor as yourself."

Preach the Law

In writing to the Corinthian church, Paul warns his readers that many will not inherit the kingdom of God, including those who violate the Law:

> Do you not know that the unrighteous will not inherit the kingdom of God? Do not be deceived. Neither fornicators, nor idolaters, nor adulterers, nor homosexuals, nor sodomites, nor thieves, nor covetous, nor drunkards, nor revilers, nor extortioners will inherit the kingdom of God. (1 Corinthians 6:9,10)

---

[58] Seventh Commandment.
[59] Sixth Commandment.
[60] Eighth Commandment.
[61] Ninth Commandment.
[62] Tenth Commandment.

Again, notice how Paul is using the Law evangelistically to bring the knowledge of sin. Those who will not enter the kingdom of God include fornicators,[63] idolaters,[64] adulterers,[65] thieves,[66] and the covetous.[67]

John Bunyan writes of this passage,

> When the apostle had told the Corinthians that the unrighteous should not inherit the kingdom of God, and that such were some of them, he adds, "But ye are washed, but ye are sanctified, but ye are justified in the name of the Lord Jesus, and by the Spirit of our God," 1 Corinthians 6:9–11; closely concluding, that had they not been washed, and sanctified, and justified, in the name of the Lord Jesus, the Law, for their transgressions, would have kept them out; it would have made the gate too strait for them to enter in.

When Paul lists the works of the flesh in Galatians chapter 5, he likewise cites the Law: adultery,[68] fornication,[69] idolatry,[70] hatred,[71] and murder[72] (verses 19,20).

---

63 Seventh Commandment.
64 Second Commandment.
65 Seventh Commandment.
66 Eighth Commandment.
67 Tenth Commandment.
68 Seventh Commandment.
69 Seventh Commandment.
70 Second Commandment.
71 Eighth Commandment.
72 Eighth Commandment.

When writing to the Ephesians, he lists fornicators[73] and the covetous[74] as those who will not inherit the kingdom of God. He even links the Tenth Commandment about coveting with the Second (idolatry) and preaches future punishment, warning of the coming wrath of God on those who do such things (see Ephesians 5:5,6).

Then Paul uses the Law evangelistically to instruct children. He addresses them specifically, and quotes the Fifth Commandment:

> "Honor your father and mother," which is the first commandment with promise: "that it may be well with you and you may live long on the earth." (Ephesians 6:2,3)

Why would Paul quote the Fifth Commandment? Was he teaching children to obey the Law? Was he telling them that they would be justified and therefore go to heaven if they kept that Commandment? Of course not. He was using it to bring the knowledge of sin. That's what he said was the purpose of the Law. Therefore, those who want to bring their children to Christ in true repentance must do the same— use the Law to bring the knowledge of sin.[75]

When Paul speaks of the power of sin, he says that "the strength of sin is the law" (1 Corinthians 15:56). If we want

---

[73] Seventh Commandment.
[74] Tenth Commandment.
[75] To help you do this, we suggest *How to Bring Your Children to Christ ... & Keep Them There* by Ray Comfort (Genesis Publishing Group).

to strengthen our case against sin and its deadly power so that sinners will turn to the Savior, we must use the Law as Paul did.

John Wesley says,

> Although there is no command in Scripture to offer Christ to the careless sinner, yet are there not scriptural precedents for it? I think not: I know not any. I believe you cannot produce one, either from the four Evangelists, or the Acts of the Apostles. Neither can you prove this to have been the practice of any of the Apostles, from any passage in all their writings.
>
> Nay, does not the Apostle Paul say, in his former Epistle to the Corinthians, "We preach Christ crucified?" (1:23) and in his latter, "We preach not ourselves, but Christ Jesus the Lord?" (4:5)
>
> We consent to rest the cause on this issue; to tread in his steps, to follow his example. Only preach you just as Paul preached, and the dispute is at an end.
>
> For although we are certain he preached Christ in as perfect a manner as the very chief of the Apostle, yet who preached the law more than St. Paul? Therefore he did not think the gospel answered the same end.[76]

"Who preached the law more than St. Paul? Therefore he did not think the gospel answered the same end."

---

[76] John Wesley, "The Law Established Through Faith," Sermon 35 <http://gbgm-umc.org/umhistory/wesley/sermons/serm-035.stm>.

Do the Work of an Evangelist

When Paul wrote to Timothy, he instructed the young pastor about the proper, "lawful" use of the Law, in light of the "glorious gospel" that has been entrusted to him:

> But we know that the law is good if one uses it lawfully, knowing this: that the law is not made for a righteous person, but for the lawless and insubordinate, for the ungodly and for sinners, for the unholy and profane, for murderers[77] of fathers and murderers of mothers, for manslayers, for fornicators,[78] for sodomites,[79] for kidnappers, for liars,[80] for perjurers, and if there is any other thing that is contrary to sound doctrine,[81] according to the glorious gospel of the blessed God which was committed to my trust. (1 Timothy 1:8–11)

Again, is Paul referring here to the Old Testament when he says "Law"? I don't believe so. In *The Bible Knowledge*

---

[77] Sixth Commandment.

[78] Seventh Commandment. Some maintain that the Ten Commandments condemn only adultery, but this verse shows that the Law also prohibits fornication—sex before marriage.

[79] The Law was made for homosexuals. It reveals that they are guilty of breaking God's Law, and are damned *despite* their sexual preference. See "The Way of the Master" episode titled "How to Witness to Someone Who is Gay," available from www.livingwaters.com.

[80] Some insist that the Ninth Commandment, "You shall not bear false witness," condemns only lying in a court of law. However, these verses show that it includes both lying and perjury.

[81] The Law condemns *all* sin.

Commentary, John Walvoord and Roy Zuck detail Paul's use of the Ten Commandments in this passage:

> *The Law* is designed to show people their sinfulness. Thus the Law is not for one who had already recognized his sin and turned to Christ. That person is no longer under the Law but should now walk in the Spirit (Gal. 5:13-26). The Law is intended for those who remain unconvinced of their sin.
>
> Paul provided a striking list of examples which seem to be intentionally based on the Ten Commandments (cf. Ex. 20:3-17). The list begins with three pairs corresponding to the first table of the Decalogue dealing with offenses against God: (1) *lawbreakers and rebels*, (2) *the ungodly and sinful*, (3) *the unholy...and irreligious...*
>
> Paul then listed violators of the first five commandments of the second table of the Decalogue: *those who kill their fathers or mothers* represent the ultimate violation of the fifth commandment, and *murderers* the sixth. *Adulterers and perverts* pertain to the seventh commandment, which was generally broadly interpreted to include all forms of sexual sin. *Slave traders* may correspond to the eighth commandment since kidnapping was viewed as the ultimate act of stealing (Ex. 21:16; Deut. 24:7). *Liars and perjurers* clearly pertain to the ninth commandment. Only the 10th commandment ("You shall not covet") is not included (but cf. Rom. 7:7). Paul concluded this inventory of

sinners with an all-inclusive reference to any behavior
which *is contrary to sound doctrine...*, including no
doubt the very behavior of the false teachers themselves.[82]

Paul also warns Timothy about signs of the last days, saying: "For men will be lovers of themselves, lovers of money
[covetous],[83] boasters, proud, blasphemers,[84] disobedient
to parents,[85] unthankful, unholy, unloving, unforgiving,
slanderers,[86] without self-control, brutal, despisers of good,
traitors, headstrong, haughty, lovers of pleasure rather than
lovers of God"[87] (2 Timothy 3:2,3). This aligns with what
Jesus said about the last days. He warned, "And because lawlessness will abound, the love of many will grow cold" (Matthew 24:12). The word "lawlessness" is a direct reference to
disregard of the moral Law.

Then Paul speaks further of these times, perfectly sum-
ming up the modern lust-filled, daytime soap operas: "For
of this sort are those who creep into households and make
captives of gullible women loaded down with sins, led away
by various lusts"[88] (2 Timothy 3:6).

---

[82] John F. Walvoord and Roy B. Zuck, *The Bible Knowledge Commen-
      tary: An Exposition of the Scriptures* (Wheaton, IL: Victor Books,
      1985).
[83] Tenth Commandment.
[84] Third Commandment.
[85] Fifth Commandment.
[86] Ninth Commandment.
[87] First Commandment.
[88] Seventh and Tenth Commandments.

How applicable this Scripture is for our time. Many of our churches are filled with teachers who don't want to speak truthfully about sin and offend their listeners. They are there because people want to think that they have an entrance to heaven and yet still enjoy the pleasures of sin—especially sexual lust: "For the time will come when they will not endure sound doctrine, but according to their own desires, because they have itching ears, they will heap up for themselves teachers; and they will turn their ears away from the truth, and be turned aside to fables" (2 Timothy 4:3,4). Many popular preachers in the contemporary Church are "seeker-friendly" by avoiding the very words that sinners need to hear to awaken them to their plight.

Paul concludes his warning with an exhortation: "But you be watchful in all things, endure afflictions, do the work of an evangelist, fulfill your ministry" (2 Timothy 4:5). What a fitting exhortation. What is the work of an evangelist? It is simply to be faithful to our calling...to do what Jesus did.

In Chapter 7, we will considering the life and words of Stephen, the first martyr for Christ, to see how he used the moral Law.

Chapter Seven

WHAT DID STEPHEN DO?

I t's amazing how our human nature leads us to see sin in others, but rarely in ourselves. Any marriage counselor can verify that spouses in contention are perpetual finger-pointers.

After having gone through the Law with thousands of people from all walks of life, I have found that they will admit to lying, but will adamantly refuse to call themselves "a liar." Experience has taught me how I can help them. I simply say, "If *I* told a lie, what would you call me?" Almost every time, "A liar!" quickly makes its way through what, only a moment before, were closed lips. We can see an example of this truth in Scripture.

The Bible tells us that Stephen was full of faith and power, doing "great wonders and signs among the people" (Acts 6:8). Many in the contemporary Church profess to do the same, but the difference is that they usually do their great wonders and signs in a musically enhanced, *controlled* environment. How much better it would be to follow the example of Jesus and Stephen and go into the marketplace, *among the people*. But be warned: an uncontrolled environment is filled with risks. Miracles are open to scrutiny from skeptics. Persecution becomes possible. Contentious fingers start pointing.

That's what happened with Stephen. When certain Jews were unable to resist the wisdom and the Spirit by which Stephen spoke, they bribed men to lie about him, stirred up a hornet's nest, and brought him before the council of the Jews.

The council wasn't concerned about the truth. They didn't search the Scriptures to see if the things that Stephen said were so. They were self-righteous, gnat-swallowing, white-washed hypocrites, who pointed a condemning finger at a man whose face looked like that of an angel (Acts 6:15). Blind to their own sin, they accused Stephen of transgressing God's Law by speaking blasphemous words. When the high priest asked him, "Are these things so?" this faithful open-air preacher was ready with an answer.

Stephen began by giving an overview of Israel's history. He spoke of Abraham, Isaac, and Joseph. Then he reminded them that Moses had transgressed the Law of God by committing murder (Acts 7:28), and that an angel of the Lord appeared to him in the wilderness of Mount Sinai. He said that God told Moses to take off his sandals because the place on which he stood was holy ground. Then Stephen recapped how God delivered their forefathers and how Israel had received the Ten Commandments, "the living oracles," on Mount Sinai. Stephen tells his hearers that God gave His Law to Moses, but their ancestors violated it with their idolatry:

> "...whom our fathers would not obey, but rejected. And in their hearts they turned back to Egypt, saying to Aaron, 'Make us gods[89] to go before us; as for this Moses who brought us out of the land of Egypt, we do not know what has become of him.' And they made a calf in those days, offered sacrifices to the idol,[90] and rejoiced in the works of their own hands." (Acts 7:39–41)

Israel incessantly transgressed the First and Second Commandments. They refused to obey God, and instead created a god to suit themselves. Human nature hasn't changed through the ages. People today still bend toward idolatry like a crooked arrow in a crooked bow.

---

[89] First Commandment.
[90] Second Commandment.

Stephen then reminded his hearers that God is not an idol, dwelling in temples made with hands, but that heaven is His throne and the earth is His footstool. By His hand He created all these things.

Compare Stephen's words to modern evangelism's vocabulary, carefully crafted not to offend its hearers. He said,

> "You stiffnecked and uncircumcised in heart and ears! You always resist the Holy Spirit; as your fathers did, so do you. Which of the prophets did your fathers not persecute? And they have killed those who foretold the coming of the Just One, of whom you now have become the betrayers and murderers,[91] who have received the law by the direction of angels and have not kept it." (Acts 7:51–53)

Before you are tempted to think that perhaps Stephen's words should have been gentler and then he may have received a different response, consider what Jesus said to His disciples. He told them that when they were brought before the authorities, they were not to worry about how to answer, because the Holy Spirit would teach them at that time what to say (Luke 12:11). So we should be careful of criticizing the content of Stephen's sermon, as we may be criticizing God Himself.

Stephen was sensitive—but his sensitivity wasn't to seekers; he was sensitive only to the will of God. His inspired

---

[91] Sixth Commandment.

words were the truth. Whether or not his hearers were of-fended by these words was secondary. It was God who was *greatly* offended by their hypocrisy. All biblical evangelistic preaching should explain that God is offended and angered by sin. If we care about the lost, we must stir the consciences of hardhearted sinners and alarm them about their danger.

Jesus rebuked His disciples for having a merciless atti-tude with no concern about warning the unsaved. When they wanted to call down fire from heaven to destroy those who didn't welcome Him, He said that they didn't know the manner of spirit in which they spoke (Luke 9:54,55). Stephen knew that, without the mercy of God, the hyp-ocrites to whom he spoke would end up in the Lake of Fire. If he didn't care about their eternal destinies, he could have tickled their ears with gentle, carefully chosen words, and he no doubt would have lived on to continue a successful and popular ministry.

Instead, he accused them of transgressing the Sixth Com-mandment—they had committed murder. God gave them the Law, and they hadn't kept it. Stephen didn't woo his lis-teners or address a God-shaped hole in their hearts. Again, he didn't carefully craft his words to avoid causing offense.

To bring sinners the knowledge of their sin and lead them to the Savior, we must not compromise the life-giving gospel. Charles Spurgeon warns,

> Avoid a sugared gospel as you would shun sugar
> of lead. Seek that gospel which rips up and tears and

cuts and wounds and hacks and even kills, for that is the gospel that makes alive again. And when you have found it, give good heed to it. Let it enter into your inmost being. As the rains soaks into the ground, so pray the Lord to let His gospel soak into your soul.

No doubt, if Stephen's hearers had admitted that they had sinned against God, and cried, "What should we do to be saved?" Stephen would have joyfully given them the good news of the gospel. But they didn't do that. Instead, his hearers were "cut to the heart, and they gnashed at him with their teeth" (Acts 7:54).

Stephen was stoned to death for preaching the uncompromising truth. He was hated for what he said. He received the scowl of man, but the smile of heaven. He followed in the bloodied footprints of his Lord and Savior. He did what Jesus did.

Stephen was the first martyr, but Peter also boldly preached the gospel, and he too died for his faith. In the next chapter, we will see how Peter used the Law to bring people to Christ.

Chapter Eight

WHAT DID PETER DO?

P eter was probably the most colorful of the disciples. He certainly was outspoken. As a leading character in the Gospels and in the Book of Acts, he was among the disciples when Jesus promised them that they would receive "power" to be witnesses of the Savior. Along with the others, he saw the breathtaking ascension and heard the angels question why they were gazing up into heaven (see Acts 1:11). They had been given the greatest of all commissions: to take the words of eternal life to a world that was sitting in the shadow of death. The angels knew that the disciples had eternity to gaze into the glories of heaven, but such a short time to speak the words of life to a sinful, dying world.

Peter was present when the disciples were filled with the promised Holy Spirit, giving them the power to be witnesses. Thank God he didn't suggest that they build three tabernacles and stay in the upper room for an endless time of worship. He remembered the thunder of God's voice telling him to *listen* to His beloved Son. Peter knew that Jesus didn't tell them to stay; *He told them to "Go."* He commanded them to "preach the gospel to every creature" (Mark 16:15). The power from on high wasn't given primarily to worship; it was given to *witness.* Jesus said, "You will receive power... and you will be My *witnesses*" (Acts 1:8, emphasis added).

Worship comes easily to those who have seen the love of the cross. It's as natural to worship the Lord as it is for a flower to open in the warmth of the summer sun. But *witnessing* isn't so easy. It's *un*natural. Witnessing is as natural to us as it is for a flower to open in the blackness of a winter's night. That's why we need the *supernatural* power of the Holy Spirit. On the Day of Pentecost, that once reticent flower did open in a cold and dark world, and the gospel was preached to thousands.

Some, however, have weighed Peter's Pentecost sermon on what they think are the balances of biblical theology, and found it greatly wanting. Consider these revealing words from a booklet called *Catching Men* by the respected Chinese author and preacher, Watchman Nee (1903–1972):

After I was saved I used to feel very dissatisfied with Peter's sermon on the day of Pentecost. Indeed I thought it was in some respects a very poor one, for it seemed so inadequate for its purpose. It did not, I thought, make things clear at all, for there is nothing in it about the plan of redemption. What does Peter say? "Jesus of Nazareth, a man approved of God unto you by mighty works and wonders and signs, which God did by him in the midst of you, even as ye yourselves know; him, being delivered up by the determinate counsel and foreknowledge of God, ye by the hand of lawless men did crucify and slay: whom God raised up..." Surely, I felt, here was the golden opportunity Peter needed to press the point home. Surely here was the time to introduce some reference to Isaiah 53, or otherwise to explain the doctrine of the atonement. But no, he let the opportunity pass, and went on: "Let all the house of Israel therefore know assuredly, that God hath made him both Lord and Christ, this Jesus whom ye crucified." How strange that Peter did not even use the title "Savior"! But nevertheless, what was the result? The people, we are told, were pricked in their heart, and cried, "What shall we do?'"

Surely it becomes clear from this that salvation is not initially a question of knowledge but of "touch." All who touch the Lord receive life. We might say that, judged by his sermons in the Acts, even Paul was not clear in his Gospel. Those many years ago the Gospel was not preached as it is now! There was not the same clear presentation of truth! But is it the truth, which is the most important? The great weakness of the present preaching of the Gospel is that we try to make people *understand* the plan of salvation, or we try to drive people to the Lord through the fear of sin and its consequences. Wherein have we failed? I am sure it is in this, that our hearers do not see *Him*, for we do not adequately present the Person. They only see "sin" or "salvation," whereas their need is to see the Lord Jesus Himself, and to meet Him and "touch" Him.

Read his words again: "Very poor...so inadequate...he let the opportunity pass...Those many years ago the Gospel was not preached as it is now! There was not the same clear presentation of truth!" It appears that he thinks Peter and the rest of the early Church need to sit at the feet of modern evangelism and learn how to clearly present the gospel.

While it is true that each of us need to "touch" Jesus, this sincere brother, like many others today, failed to understand to whom Peter was speaking. As I mentioned previously, no sensible farmer would cast good seed onto hard soil. He first breaks up the soil, removes the stones, etc., and then he plants good seed onto good soil. The soil upon which Peter sowed had been prepared by the Law.

A. W. Pink says,

> Just as the world was not ready for the New Testament before it received the Old, just as the Jews were

not prepared for the ministry of Christ until John the Baptist had gone before Him with his claimant call to repentance, so the unsaved are in no condition today for the Gospel till the Law be applied to their hearts, for "by the Law is the knowledge of sin." It is a waste of time to sow seed on ground which has never been ploughed or spaded! To present the vicarious sacrifice of Christ to those whose dominant passion is to take fill of sin, is to give that which is holy to the dogs.[92]

On the Day of Pentecost, Peter was speaking to "Jews, devout men" (Acts 2:5). These were godly men who knew *from the Law* that sin was "exceedingly sinful." They knew that they were under God's wrath. They knew the righteousness, holiness, and justice of God—because the Law taught them. It gave them the "knowledge of sin" (Romans 3:20) and was their "schoolmaster to bring [them] to Christ" (Galatians 3:24, KJV). These were sinners whose stony hearts had been prepared by the Law for the pure seed of the gospel. So when Peter stood up to speak, he didn't need to preach doctrines that would convince his hearers that they needed the Savior. They already knew that. Peter simply sowed the good seed of the gospel on the good soil of their prepared hearts. He preached Christ crucified and the result was that three thousand souls were saved (Acts 2:41).

---

[92] A. W. Pink, *Studies on Saving Faith* <http://www.reformed.org/books/pink/saving_faith/saving_faith_1_01.html>.

Some Christians believe that unregenerate *Gentiles* simply need to hear the same message that Peter gave to awaken them. So they make the mistake of sowing the seed without preparing the soil. They are often sincere, kind, loving, Christ-centered, Bible-believing Christians, but they are unaware of the important principle of *biblical* evangelism: Law to the proud, grace to the humble. They fail to see the need for the Law to do its work in preparing the heart for grace, and the result is that the Church has been filled with false converts—as shown by the massive fall-away rate[93] in their "converts."

Notice again that Scripture makes clear the "soil" upon which Peter was sowing: "Men of Israel" (Acts 2:22), "Let all the house of Israel know..." (verse 36). When he preached in Solomon's porch, Peter was speaking in the temple to Jews who obviously knew the Law; he called them "men of Israel" and preached Christ crucified (see Acts 3:12–26). He climaxed by telling them that God sent Jesus to turn away "every one of you from your iniquities" (verse 26). Once again, the word "iniquities" (lawlessness) is a direct reference to transgression of the moral Law. Peter, in his Pentecost sermon, also mentioned the fact that his hearers had violated the Law: "[Him] you have taken by lawless hand, have crucified and put to death; whom God raised up..." (Acts 2:23, 24).

---

[93] See *The Way of the Master* by Kirk Cameron and Ray Comfort (Tyndale House Publishers).

Peter and Persecution

Peter first tasted persecution when he "preached in Jesus the resurrection from the dead" (Acts 4:2,3). The world doesn't mind hearing about the Jesus in a manger, but the One who will come in wrath and judge in righteousness is not so cuddly. It's not as easy to snuggle up to a Savior who will return in flaming fire (2 Thessalonians 1:8). Nevertheless, Peter—who earlier denied that he even knew Jesus—was now filled with the Holy Spirit (Acts 4:8) and boldly told them that Jesus was the only means by which anyone could be saved (verse 12). When Peter and John were strongly encouraged to become "seeker-friendly" by removing the name of Jesus from their vocabulary, they refused (verses 19,20).

Peter and Cornelius

Watchman Nee was also disturbed by what he perceived to be the shallow nature of Peter's preaching to Cornelius and his friends. He lamented,

> Later on Peter went to Gentiles who had a different religious background altogether. There surely, you feel, the Gospel would be plainly preached. Yet to Cornelius Peter only spoke about who Christ was, and though he certainly mentioned the remission of sins he gave no explanation of the meaning of His death— yet even so, the Holy Spirit fell upon them all.

Again, look at his words: "Gentiles who had a different religious background altogether." They were Gentiles, *but they didn't have a different background.* As we've seen, Jews were given the Law written in stone, but all of humanity has the Law written on their hearts.

Consider the "soil" upon which Peter was about to sow. Cornelius was a *just* man who *feared God.* He had a good reputation among the Jews and had been spoken to directly by an angel (see Acts 10:22). He was humble of heart and had been fasting and praying (verses 25,30). This was thoroughly prepared soil. Something had caused Cornelius to thirst for the righteousness of God, which implies that he had a knowledge of sin. Peter therefore preached Christ crucified, the resurrection, Judgment Day, and the universal offer of the forgiveness of sins (verses 36–43). While Mr. Nee may not be pleased with Peter's words, the Holy Spirit was pleased enough to fall upon his hearers.

To imply that Peter's sermon lacked the essential truths of the gospel, but God saved three thousand at Pentecost anyway, would mean that God isn't too concerned with truth. If we believe Peter's words lacked crucial truths at the house of Cornelius, but God saved the hearers anyway, why then should any of us get upset if someone omits essential truths? This is why Mr. Nee asked, "But is it the truth, which is the most important? God will save sinners anyway." Perhaps this is why so many have strayed from the truths essential to biblical evangelism and are not concerned about it. But in reality, the truth wasn't compromised. Rather, the soil of their hearts had already been prepared.

Peter and Ananias and Sapphira

In Acts chapter 5, a covetous husband and wife decided that they would break the Ninth and Tenth Commandments. Their attitude revealed that they were also breaking the First and Second Commandments in not putting God first. They obviously lacked a healthy fear of God, and those who have no fear of God have an erroneous image of Him.

Peter confronted the couple with the fact that they had violated the Ninth Commandment by lying, not just to men but to God. Their judgment was swift, showing that what we may consider an inconsequential sin God takes very seriously (see Acts 5:1–10).

No stranger to confrontation, Peter soon found himself tackling Simon the sorcerer (see Acts 8:5–24). Simon believed, was baptized, and loved the "power gifts." However, he was a *false* convert. The Scriptures tell us that his heart wasn't right with God; he was unrepentant, wicked, bitter, and still "bound by iniquity" (verses 21–23). Like the lying and covetous couple (and many others nowadays who profess faith in Jesus), he ignored the Commandments. Simon "believed," but still transgressed the Law of God—and Peter didn't hesitate to tell him so.

I am often asked what to say to "Christians" whose lifestyles exemplify a false conversion. I suggest giving them the audio message "Hell's Best Kept Secret."[94] When you hand

---

[94] This can be purchased on a CD at www.livingwaters.com or can be freely downloaded from the site (it is non-copyrighted).

someone the CD, say, "I need to know what you think of this." That gives them a sense of obligation. You are not lying when you say this; you do need to know their thoughts.

Although Peter made few direct references to the Law, we must remember that his ministry was intended only for the Jews (see Galatians 2:7,8)—those who knew the Law and understood their state before God. They didn't need to be awakened by the Law to see their need for mercy. Paul's ministry was to the Gentiles, and we therefore see many references to the Law in his life and in his teachings.

Consider again the words of Watchman Nee (which are typical of the modern church):

> The great weakness of the present preaching of the Gospel is that we try to make people *understand* the plan of salvation, or we try to drive people to the Lord through the fear of sin and its consequences.

With due respect, the exact opposite is true. As Charles Spurgeon said, "If people are to be saved by a message, it must contain at least some measure of knowledge. There must be light as well as fire." The great *weakness* of the present preaching of the gospel is that people *don't* understand the plan of salvation. They don't think they need a Savior to save them from the coming wrath—the just punishment for sin— because the Law hasn't been used to *show* them their sins.

If you aren't convinced of this, then ask a sinner if he thinks he is a good person. He will almost always adamantly testify to his own righteousness. The lost seek to establish their own righteousness, being ignorant of the righteousness of God (see Romans 10:3). It is because of this that so few are driven to the Savior through the fear of sin's eternal consequences, and therefore end up in the same plight as Simon the sorcerer—professing Christians who, in reality, are still "bound by iniquity." They say that they believe in Jesus but they continue to violate the Ten Commandments by lying, stealing, lusting, etc., as "workers of iniquity."

The consequences of sin are to be greatly feared. Proverbs 16:6 tells us, "In mercy and truth atonement is provided for iniquity [lawlessness]; and *by the fear of the LORD one departs from evil*" (emphasis added).

Remember, the Scriptures were given for our instruction. We are to learn from them. So, may we sit at the feet of the early Church and learn the powerful lesson of knowing the soil upon which we are about to sow.

The Oracles of God

In 1 Peter 4:11, Peter states, "If anyone speaks, let him speak as the oracles of God." What specifically are the "oracles of God"? Stephen tells us in Acts 7:38. He says, "This is he who was in the congregation in the wilderness with the Angel who spoke to him on Mount Sinai, and with our fathers, the one who received the living oracles to give to us." The living oracles were given to Moses on Mount Sinai, which is a specific reference to the moral Law.

Paul also mentions the oracles of God in the Book of Romans. Asking if the Jew has any advantage, he answers,

"Much in every way! Chiefly because to them were committed the oracles of God" (Romans 3:2). The words "oracles of God" obviously refer to the moral Law. As we have seen, any Jew who has knowledge of the Law has the advantage of knowing the nature of sin. He knows the standards of God, and therefore should regard sin as being exceedingly sinful.

The author of the Book of Hebrews also makes reference to "the oracles of God." He says, "For though by this time you ought to be teachers, you need someone to teach you again the first principles of the oracles of God; and you have come to need milk and not solid food" (Hebrews 5:12). The moral Law is the foundation upon which sound doctrine stands. We ought to be teachers, teaching the Law to sinners. After David had confessed his transgressions of the moral Law to God, he said, "Then I will teach transgressors Your ways, and sinners shall be converted to You" (Psalm 51:13).

Jesus spoke of the greatness of those who taught the Law, saying, "Whoever therefore breaks one of the least of these commandments, and teaches men so, shall be called least in the kingdom of heaven; but whoever does and teaches them, he shall be called great in the kingdom of heaven" (Matthew 5:19).

So if you want to do what Jesus did and be great in the kingdom of God, teach transgressors—by telling them what they have transgressed.

WHAT DID JAMES DO?

It's easy to read through the Book of James and overlook his consistent use of the Law. As with Jesus and Paul, James regularly preached its precepts and was faithful to warn of future punishment.

He begins his letter by informing his hearers that when we sin, we are drawn away by our own lusts (see James 1:14, KJV). Lust is transgression of the Seventh and Tenth Commandments. He tells us that lust gives birth to sin, and sin when it is full-grown brings forth death. Then he warns, "Do not be deceived, my beloved brethren" (verse 16). Lust is *deceiving*. It removes eternity from the eyes. It wants immediate pleasure, despite the terrible eternal consequences. For the love of lust a man will turn his back on a faithful wife. Lust will draw him into adultery, with no regard for his children, his good name, or his God.

James warns that lust will deceive a professing Christian and cause him to live in hypocrisy. He tells his readers to "be doers of the word, and not hearers only, deceiving yourselves" (James 1:22). Then he tells us what awakens a sinner to the deceptive nature of sin. He explains that it is the Law of God, likening it to a mirror:

> For if anyone is a hearer of the word and not a doer, he is like a man observing his natural face in a mirror; for he observes himself, goes away, and immediately forgets what kind of man he was. But he who looks into the perfect law of liberty and continues in it, and is not a forgetful hearer but a doer of the work, this one will be blessed in what he does. (James 1:23–25)

Mirrors tell us when we need cleansing, and that is what the Law does. It reflects what we are in truth. When Paul was deceived by sin, it was the mirror of the Commandment that showed him its deception. Seeing his true image reflected in the mirror of the Law revealed to Paul that he was unclean and condemned:

> And the commandment, which was to bring life, I found to bring death. For sin, taking occasion by the commandment, deceived me, and by it killed me.

Therefore the law is holy, and the commandment holy and just and good. (Romans 7:10–12)

In verse 25, is James speaking of the entire Old Testament when he refers to "the perfect law of liberty"? I don't believe so because just a few verses later he refers to the Law as the "royal law":

If you really fulfill the royal law according to the Scripture, "You shall love your neighbor as yourself," you do well; but if you show partiality, you commit sin, and are convicted by the law as transgressors. (James 2:8,9)

In calling the Law "royal" (verse 8), James reminds us that this is the Law of the King of kings—there is no higher law than the Law of Almighty God.

James and Future Punishment

When James spoke of how we often show partiality to the rich and ignore the poor, he reminded his hearers that the rich they so admire transgress the Third Commandment by blaspheming God's holy name (James 2:7). If we show partiality, or fail to love our neighbor as much as we love ourselves, we transgress the Law's precepts. We are then *convicted* by it (James 2:9). It charges us as guilty, and without the Savior we will remain under its terrible wrath until its fury comes upon us.

Is James saying that we should love our neighbor as ourselves so that we can go to heaven? Is he preaching justification by the Law? Of course not. Scripture tells us clearly that "a man is not justified by the works of the law but by faith in Jesus Christ" (Galatians 2:16). The Law was made for the lawless and disobedient. James is using the Law *evangelistically*—for the purpose for which it was designed (see 1 Timothy 1:8–10).

James then warns that if we transgress even one part of the Law, we are guilty of breaking the whole Law (see James 2:10). This is an important point to bring out when witnessing. Most people believe they're pretty good if they haven't broken *all* the Commandments. But this verse makes it clear that against the holy standard of God's perfect Law, absolute perfection is required. Breaking even *one* Law is sufficient to declare a sinner guilty—just as if he's broken all of them.

As with Paul, James becomes specific when he speaks of "the Law." It couldn't be clearer that it was the moral Law— the Ten Commandments—because he then quotes the Commandments in conjunction with future punishment:

> For He who said, "Do not commit adultery,"[95] said also, "Do not murder."[96] Now if you do not commit adultery, but you do murder, you have become a transgressor of the law. So speak and so do as those who will be judged by the law of liberty. (James 2:11,12)

Why would he use the Law and threaten future punishment if he was writing to Christians? James is using the Law

---

[95] Seventh Commandment.
[96] Sixth Commandment.

evangelistically—both to bring the knowledge of sin to sinners and to instruct Christians on how to do the same, because Scripture is given for our instruction (2 Timothy 3:16). He informs us that the Law is the righteous standard by which God will judge the world. This is also what Paul tells us in Romans 2:12: "as many as have sinned in the law will be judged by the law."

In verse 19 James reminds his hearers of the essence of the First Commandment—that there is one God, and that to *believe* in Him means more than just an intellectual assent to His existence. Even the demons believe, and tremble at the very thought of the One the Bible says is a consuming fire.

However, spiritually blind sinners blaspheme His name. In James 3:6, Scripture calls the blasphemous tongue a "world of iniquity" [lawlessness]. We are told in Romans 8:7 that the mind of unregenerate men is in a state of hostility toward God. Notice where the hostility is directed: the carnal mind "*is not subject to the law of God*, nor indeed can be" (emphasis added). The tongue is the willing mouthpiece of a hostile mind that hates God's Law.

The Cause of Wars

Notice that James is writing to "the twelve tribes which are scattered abroad" (James 1:1). While much of his epistle is directed to Christians, he cannot forget the unsaved who are among them. If you think that the "tribes" are all sanctified saints, look at the lifestyles he accuses them of living.

He asks where the wars and fighting among them come from, and quickly answers that they come from their evil desires. He accuses them of murder,[97] coveting,[98] and adultery,[99] and tells them that friendship with this sinful world makes them enemies of God (James 4:1–4). His words are not a good blueprint for seeker-friendly sermons.

He uses the Law to bring the knowledge of sin, then he informs his proud and self-righteous hearers that God *resists* them, but He gives grace to the humble (verse 6). Again, biblical evangelism follows the principle of "Law to the proud and grace to the humble." With the Law we break the hard heart; with the gospel we heal the broken one.

James informs his proud and self-righteous hearers that God resists them, but He gives grace to the humble.

James then explains that God is not their "friend" (as sinners are often told), and that if they want to live, they must submit to His will (verse 7). He further reveals that he is preaching to the soil of proud, unsaved people, by calling them "sinners" and telling them to *humble* themselves:

> Draw near to God and He will draw near to you. Cleanse your hands, you sinners; and purify your hearts, you double-minded. Lament and mourn and

---

97 Sixth Commandment.
98 Tenth Commandment.
99 Seventh Commandment.

weep! Let your laughter be turned to mourning and your joy to gloom. Humble yourselves in the sight of the Lord, and He will lift you up. (James 4:8–10)

If they will draw near to God, He will draw near to them. If they are willing to come to Him in surrender, He is willing to negotiate peace, as Isaiah tells us:

"Come now, and let us reason together," says the LORD, "Though your sins are like scarlet, they shall be as white as snow; though they are red like crimson, they shall be as wool." (Isaiah 1:18)

How do you convince the lost, who think they are already as white as snow, that they need forgiveness? Simply uphold the standard of pure white righteousness next to their darkened, sinful heart. Omit the Law and sinners will continue to think that they have peace with God. But they have defiled their hands through sin, and they must purify their hearts through the blood of the Savior: "Who may ascend into the hill of the LORD? . . . He who has clean hands and a pure heart" (Psalm 24:3,4).

The only way they can find peace with God is to "lament and mourn and weep" (James 4:9); these things are the outworkings of a genuinely repentant heart. If there is no godly sorrow, there is no repentance. The Scriptures tell us that it is godly sorrow that produces repentance to salvation (see 2 Corinthians 7:10). How then can sin-loving men and women come to a place of "mourning" and "gloom" over that which gives them laughter and joy? Only by the grace of God.

Isaiah called God "our Lawgiver." He said, "For the LORD is our Judge, the LORD is our Lawgiver, the LORD is our King; He will save us" (Isaiah 33:22). James makes a similar statement: "There is one Lawgiver, who is able to save and to destroy" (James 4:12).

When we too preach that there is one Lawgiver who is able to save and to destroy, sinners can begin to understand the cross—that Christ died for us while we were yet sinners. It is there that a hard, sin-loving heart becomes tender. At the foot of a bloodstained cross, a godless world can see His love and mercy. There they find a place of contrition. The Judge of the Universe can save them through His mercy, or destroy them through His fearful justice. Those who see the mercy of the cross, understanding that justice calls for their blood, will see it through tear-filled eyes.

There is a big difference between *contrition* (being sorry *for* your sin) and *regret* (being sorry because *you are caught* in sin). It is the thorough use (and understanding of) the Law that is a great factor in determining the difference. Those who are merely sorry that they were caught never see that their condemnation is just. In the Parable of the Sower, it is only the good soil hearer who hears and *understands* (see Matthew 13:23). The man with an understanding heart yields to the authority of His Creator. He doesn't merely say, "I have been exposed in my sin." He says, "I have been exposed in my sin, and God is justified in condemning me for it. I have sinned *against Him*."

This was the core of David's contrite prayer in Psalm 51. He had been exposed, but he justified God in his confession of guilt. He said, "Against You, You only, have I sinned, and done this evil in Your sight; that *You may be found just when You speak, and blameless when You judge*" (verse 4, emphasis added).

James has not finished using the Law. He speaks to those who love their money more than they love God,[100] warning them of future punishment (see James 5:1–3). He informs them that on that Day, their shameful sins will be a witness against them, accusing them of murder,[101] and warning that the Judge is at the door (verse 9). He then reminds them of the grace of God, telling them that this same Judge is "very compassionate and merciful" (verse 11). Again, this is the biblical principle of Law before grace, of *preparing* the soil before sowing seed.

He concludes his letter by reminding us of what happens when a sinner turns from his evil way and comes to Christ. The guilty criminal is saved from death—his death sentence is commuted and he is allowed to live.

In the next chapter, we will continue to look at the necessity of warning sinners to repent, by considering the ministry of John the Baptist.

---

[100] First Commandment.
[101] Sixth Commandment.

Chapter Ten

WHAT DID JOHN THE BAPTIST DO?

John the Baptist might find it difficult to get invitations to speak in churches today. Every pastor who entrusts his pulpit to another takes a risk. John would be a great risk. He didn't avoid offensive words such as repentance, hell, and judgment, and he referred to his hearers as snakes—not the encouraging, uplifting words often heard in contemporary churches. He didn't seem to care what his listeners thought of him. He would say things like,

> "Brood of vipers! Who warned you to flee from the wrath to come?" (Matthew 3:7)

John may not be considered a great preacher by today's standards. He did, however, have Heaven's commendation. Jesus said that out of the multitudes born into this world, John was the *greatest*. He was number one on the list that matters. Jesus said,

> "Assuredly, I say to you, among those born of wo-men there has not risen one greater than John the Bap-tist; but he who is least in the kingdom of heaven is greater than he." (Matthew 11:11)

The best of today's preachers would not be worthy to tie his shoes.

The Sharp Axe of Death

Notice that John's messages didn't hint of God's love. Instead, he preached the Law and its wrath, using the Law evangelistically.

After speaking about the wrath to come and telling his listeners (those he called "vipers") to bear fruits worthy of repentance, he warns that those not bearing good fruit will be thrown into the fire. So people then asked him, "What shall we do?" In his answers, John gave them specific examples on how to apply the essence of the Law (Luke 3:8–14).

He told King Herod that he was living in adultery.[102] The king was married, but on a trip to Rome he stopped to visit his half-brother, Philip. Herod lusted after Philip's

---

[102] Seventh Commandment.

wife, Herodias, and talked her into leaving her husband. Then he divorced his own wife, so he and Herodias could marry. As far as God was concerned, they were living in adultery (see Matthew 5:32). They were in transgression of the Seventh Commandment, and John confronted him about it. Scripture tells us:

> John had said to him, "It is not lawful for you to have her." (Matthew 14:4)

There are interesting parallels between John the Baptist and what we should be as Christians. Here are some of his wonderful virtues:

- He was separated from the world.

- He had no fear of man.

- He called people to repent.

- He preached future punishment.

- He was a burning and shining light.

- He had a diet of locusts and honey.

- He was humble of heart.

- He pointed to the Lamb of God.

- He told sinners to prepare the way of the Lord.

Every disciple of Christ should be like John. We should be separated from the world; we are to be in the world, but

not of it. We should have such a love for God and deep concern for the lost that we dismiss the "fear of man," and instead fear God enough to obey Him. We must call sinners
to repent of their sin. Like John, we shouldn't hesitate to
warn of the coming future punishment. We too should be a
burning and shining light, with a diet of locusts and honey
—a correct understanding of the plague of God's Law and
the sweet honey of the gospel. We must humbly point to
the suffering Lamb of God, and tell sinners to prepare their
hearts for the Lord. We are forerunners of Jesus Christ and
His Second Coming.

Not surprisingly, the people criticized John for his message, claiming that he "has a demon" (see Luke 7:33). But
that didn't deter him. As with Stephen, preaching the Law
cost John the Baptist his life (see Matthew 14:10). His ministry was cut short by the king's axe. But as he laid his neck
beneath the sharp blade, what should have been his most
fearful moment swiftly became his most glorious...be-
cause he had already died to himself. He had already given
up his life to God on the altar of sacrifice.

If the Lord tarries, the time will come when we too will
feel the sharp axe of death. But because of Calvary, what
should have been our most frightening moment will turn
into our most glorious. Until that time, we must be the
most sober of people, and like John, never compromise the
message for a moment, even if it costs us our life. All John
had to do to avoid persecution was to soften his message to
the king. There wouldn't have been offense if he had just

been more sensitive. But John wasn't concerned for himself; he was concerned for the salvation of the king. He knew Herod's fearful fate if he didn't repent.

Warning the Wicked

This sin-loving world, in its ignorance, smiles at sin. Like a rebellious child, it holds a match ready to strike a matchbox in a gas-filled room. How can we fail to warn them? Yet, many preachers today seem to have no interest in sounding the alarm. They don't see themselves as "watchmen" warning every man, that they might present every man perfect in Christ. Look at what God said to the prophet Ezekiel:

> So you, son of man: I have made you a watchman for the house of Israel; therefore you shall hear a word from My mouth and warn them for Me. When I say to the wicked, 'O wicked man, you shall surely die!' and you do not speak to warn the wicked from his way, that wicked man shall die in his iniquity; but his blood I will require at your hand. (Ezekiel 33:7,8)

Paul saw that he had a responsibility not to hold back from preaching the whole counsel of God. He said, "Therefore I testify to you this day that I am innocent of the blood of all men. For I have not shunned to declare to you the whole counsel of God" (Acts 20:26,27).

But Satan, as we've seen throughout Church history, is incredibly subtle. He has watered down the counsel of God, adulterating the message. His method has been to remove the moral Law and any talk of future punishment from the gospel of salvation, and the inevitable consequence is to remove the fear of the Lord. The message he has brought into the Church has filled it with those who assume they can enjoy the grace of God and yet continue in sin.

Another predictable tragedy when the Law and future punishment are left out of the gospel message is that it leaves the preacher without any real necessity to preach the cross. Failure to use the Law leaves both the preacher and the hearer without the dilemma of unpaid debt. That's why so many preachers simply say that sinners need to come to Jesus to find true peace, and few notice that something is missing from the message. Where is the blood of the cross? It's not mentioned because there is no *need* for it. If there's no expounded Law, showing the sinner that he's under God's wrath, that there's going to be a terrible Day of Judgment, and an everlasting hell, why then do we need the cross? Why offer water when no thirst has been created?

"Preaching that leaves out the cross is the laughing stock of hell."

How true are these words of Charles Spurgeon: "Preaching that leaves out the cross is the laughing stock of hell."

Moral Hygienist

For years, I have tried to witness to my dentist. He is very likeable, incredibly intelligent, and the most foul-mouthed man you could ever meet. He's no moral hygienist. Whenever I mention sin, he steps backward and quickly changes the subject. Yet he loves to watch a popular preacher on TV.

I decided to listen closely to this admired minister to see why my dentist enjoys his messages, and heard the pastor tell his congregation that God loved them. He told them that God valued them. God cared about them. They were special to Him. He approved of them. He wasn't at all mad at them. They were made in His image. They were God's own masterpiece and there is no one like them. God accepted them. He had a plan for them. He would never give up on them. He wasn't concerned about their weaknesses, their faults, or their mistakes. If they messed up, it didn't matter. They needed to simply ask God for forgiveness. They were of *great* value to Him.

In a thirty-minute sermon, he said fifteen to twenty times that God accepted them. He was like a preaching thesaurus, saying the same thought (that God approved of his hearers) in dozens of different ways. Obviously, every pastor should regularly speak of God's love to his flock, but something wasn't quite right with this sermon.

Why does any congregation need to be reassured of God's love? Why do they need to be told again and again of God's approval? The answer is clear: they have never seen the love of Calvary's cross. There is something wrong with a marriage relationship if someone else needs to continually reassure a wife that her husband really does love her, and that he accepts her.

At the end of this pastor's sermon, he addressed the unsaved, revealing why his congregation was so evidently insecure about God's love. He simply invited people to make Jesus the Lord of their life, mentioning peace and happiness. During a quick sinner's prayer, he did pray, "I repent of my sins," but there was no mention of the cross. Not even a hint of it. Neither was there any reference to Judgment Day, the moral Law, the need for righteousness, or the reality of hell.

No wonder my dentist likes him.

Infested Waters

There is a great difference between those who understand the cross and those who don't. The understanding comes from the knowledge of the personal nature of sin. Those who have seen their own sin in all its horror can appreciate the cross in all its glory. They whisper with the apostle, "God forbid that I should boast except in the cross of our Lord Jesus Christ..." (Galatians 6:14).

If my father gave his own life by jumping into crocodile-infested waters to save me from a certain and terrifying death, I don't need anyone to reassure me of his love. No one has to try to convince me that my dad cared about me. I have his love graphically evidenced by what he did for me. In fact, if someone told me a hundred times that my dad *really did* love me, I would wonder if that person had even heard about my father's incredible act of heroism.

In this preacher's entire thirty minutes of reassurance, not once did I hear him even mention Jesus, let alone speak of His blood shed on the cross. Yet, if he would simply take the time to open up the moral Law (the Ten Commandments) as Jesus did, and preach that God is angered by sin, but that His great love drove Him to become a Man to save us from wrath and the terrible fate of hell, he wouldn't have to constantly repeat to his congregation that God loved them. They would *know* of His fathomless love because they have seen Jesus Christ evidently set forth and crucified. Eternal justice put Him on the cross and infinite love kept Him there, and there is no greater place of security than at the foot of that blood-stained cross.

Please understand that it isn't my intent to attack the person of seeker-friendly preachers, but to point out their error of departing from biblical evangelism—*because it has devastating and fearful consequences*. I too have met this pastor and found him to be very likeable. But if a sweet elderly lady was giving out sandwiches which I knew had salmonella poisoning, the fact that she was sweet would have nothing to do with the issue. I would have to speak up and say that in her ignorance she is poisoning those to whom she is seeking to show kindness.

If you want sinners to embrace the cross, then use the Ten Commandments to help them understand their sin. Consider these words of J. C. Ryle:

I say, then, in the first place, that a scriptural view of sin is one of the best antidotes to that vague, dim, misty, hazy kind of theology which is so painfully current in the present age... Now I believe the likeliest way to cure and mend this defective kind of religion is to bring forward more prominently the old scriptural truth about the sinfulness of sin. People will never set their faces decidedly towards heaven, and live like pilgrims, until they really feel that they are in danger of hell. Let us revive the old teaching about sin, in nurseries, in schools, in training colleges, in universities. Let us not forget that "the law is good if we use it lawfully," and that "by the law is the knowledge of sin" (1 Tim. 1:8; Romans 3:20; 7:7). Let us bring the Law to the front and press it on men's attention.

The Law produces that which is "sweeter... than honey and the honeycomb" (Psalm 19:10). When you use the biting locust of the Law, the gospel that once had no taste suddenly becomes sweeter than the honeycomb.

Chapter Eleven

WHAT DID JUDE DO?

J ude begins his epistle by establishing his motivation. Like Paul, he is a "bondservant of Jesus Christ" (verse 1). That means Jesus Christ was his Lord, and he did the will of his Master. What Jesus said, Jude did. He imitated his Lord both in motivation, and in His method when reaching out to the lost.

Jude had a burning heart for the unsaved. He felt compelled to write to his hearers and exhort them to "contend earnestly for the faith." Jude's reason for the exhortation to fight was that "certain men have crept in unnoticed" and turned "the grace of our God into lewdness..." (verses 3,4). They were turning God's mercy into a license to sin. *The Amplified Bible* says that they were men "who pervert the grace (the spiritual blessing and favor) of our God into lawlessness..." In other words, they were teaching that people could be saved, and yet live in immorality, violating God's Law by lying, stealing, etc.

Jesus Loves You

A young man approached me following a church service in which I had shared "Hell's Best Kept Secret" (a message explaining the use of the Law in evangelism). He said that he used to intensely dislike my ministry and message. This was because for years he would regularly show up in Huntington Beach in Southern California with a sign that said "Jesus loves you." Christians who understood the principle of Law before grace would approach him to say that what he was doing was unbiblical, and my name would often come up in the conversation. That fueled his contempt for the teaching. But he said that after hearing "Hell's Best Kept Secret" a second time, he suddenly understood it.

Then this young man revealed something interesting. He said that before that point of understanding, he had no fear of God. He said that even while he was running around with his "Jesus loves you" message, he was still into sin. He was living the life of a hypocrite. He was Lawless, and understandably lived a lawless lifestyle. John Bunyan said, "Sin is the dare of God's justice, the jeer of His patience, the slight of His power, and the contempt of His love."

Listen as Charles Spurgeon, the Prince of Preachers, once again addresses the use of the Law in the gospel presentation:

> He who would have a fruitful ministry must have clear shining after the rain, by which I mean, first, Law, and then, gospel. We must preach plainly against sin. In our ministry there must be rain, we must have the clouds and darkness, and divine justice bearing heavily upon the sinner's conscience. Then comes in Christ crucified, full atonement, simple faith, and clear shining of comfort to the believing sinner. But there must be the rain first. *He who preaches all sweetness and all love, and has nothing to do with warning men of the consequences of sin, may be thought to be very loving; but, in truth, he is altogether unfaithful to the souls of men.* (emphasis added)

In another sermon he continues with the same theme:

> The Divine Spirit wounds before He heals, He kills before He makes alive. We usually draw a distinction between Law-work and gospel-work; but Law-work is the work of the Spirit of God, and is so far a true gospel-work that it is a frequent preliminary to the joy and peace of the gospel.

To preach the Law is to biblically "preach Christ." This is because the moral Law cannot be separated from God's character. He didn't one day think to Himself, "I will create a moral standard to separate right from wrong. Let's see … from now on it will be wrong to lie, to steal, to commit adultery, and to kill." If that happened sometime way back in eternity, then what was God's standard of morality before He had the idea to create a moral standard?

Of course, such a thought is ridiculous. The Law of God is eternal—it *cannot* be separated from His very nature. It is the heart and soul of God. This is clearly apparent in the incarnation. Ravi Zacharias said, "Take a look at the person of Christ, and in Him you will see the moral Law embodied."[103] This is why is it so wrong to divorce Him from the Law—to preach Christ without preaching the Law. The result is to turn the grace of our God into lewdness (Jude 4).

Listen to Jude's message, and compare his preaching to the uplifting, motivational speakers who stand in many modern pulpits:

> The angels who did not keep their proper domain, but left their own abode, He has reserved in everlasting chains under darkness for the judgment of the great day: as Sodom and Gomorrah, and the cities around them in a similar manner to these, having given themselves over to sexual immorality,[104] and gone after strange flesh, are set forth as an example, suffering the vengeance of eternal fire.[105] (Jude 6,7)

---

[103] Trinity Broadcasting Network interview, broadcast August 6, 2004.
[104] Seventh Commandment.
[105] Future punishment.

Jude preached about the wrath of God that fell on Sodom and Gomorrah. This is recorded as an example for us—they suffered the vengeance of eternal fire so we would fear God and not make the same terrible mistakes. Jude says these "dreamers" speak evil of things they don't understand. They are corrupt brute beasts filled with greed. Then he puts his finger on the problem: they have no fear of God (verse 12).

In Romans 3, Paul likewise spoke of the ungodly, describing them as having no understanding, being unprofitable, with deceitful tongues, full of cursing and bitterness. They were filled with violence, destruction, and misery. Then he put his finger on the problem: there was no fear of God before their eyes (verse 18). The remedy to such a state was given in the very next verse. He preached the Law of God.

Remember, Jude was speaking of those who had crept into the Church with a poisonous message. He was exposing their motive and their terrible fate. How was he doing it? By doing what Jesus did—preaching future punishment. Look at what Jude says of the ungodly:

> [They are] raging waves of the sea, foaming up their own shame; wandering stars for whom is reserved the blackness of darkness forever.[106] Now Enoch, the seventh from Adam, prophesied about these men also, saying, "Behold, the Lord comes with ten thousands of His saints, to execute judgment on all,[107] to convict all who are ungodly among them of all their ungodly

---

[106] Future punishment.
[107] Future punishment.

deeds which they have committed in an ungodly way, and of all the harsh things which ungodly sinners have spoken against Him." These are grumblers, complainers, walking according to their own lusts;[108] and they mouth great swelling words, flattering people to gain advantage. But you, beloved, remember the words which were spoken before by the apostles of our Lord Jesus Christ: how they told you that there would be mockers in the last time who would walk according to their own ungodly lusts.[109] (Jude 13–18)

In closing his epistle, Jude shows again that his passion was to seek and save the lost:

Others save with fear, pulling them out of the fire, hating even the garment defiled by the flesh. (Jude 23)

He likens Christians to firefighters. We are to reach out to those at whom the flames of eternal wrath are licking. Like Paul, Jude couples evangelism with fear. Paul said, "Knowing, therefore, the terror of the Lord, we persuade men" (2 Corinthians 5:11). We are to rescue the perishing, permeated with fear. We are fearful because of the horror of their terrible fate, and we are fearful because Almighty God commands us to such a sobering task. We dare not be passive about our commission or for one moment trifle with our message.

---

[108] Seventh and Tenth Commandments.
[109] Seventh and Tenth Commandments.

The Biblical Criteria

Occasionally I'm asked if our ministry keeps records of converts. In other words, is there any evidence proving that using the Law before grace *really* works? We don't keep records, because the only record that counts is kept by God—the Book of Life. Those who claim to know how many were saved under their message disregard any thought that there are good fish alongside the bad, or wheat among the tares.

The number of decisions made shouldn't be the criteria for judging this or any teaching. Mega churches that preach life improvement through Christian principles are numerically very successful, something that even the world acknowledges. The criteria shouldn't be, Is this successful? But, Is this teaching biblical? Is this what Jesus did?

With that said, we do receive many testimonies about the power of God's Law to bring the knowledge of sin. Consider this letter from a pastor of worship and evangelism who visited Brazil:

> I recently returned from Brazil where I shared the gospel with many people. I started with creation, telling them that God created them and everything they see, but that man rebelled against God. I told them God gave His Law to show us that we have sinned against Him, then I went through the Law one by one. In almost every home I preached in, the people were somewhat unconcerned until I went through the Law. It was so incredible. The guys who were with me noticed the same thing. They saw the "deer in the head-

lights" look on people's faces when I brought out the Law. They realized why I shared the Ten Commandments before I could explain it. They knew, simply because of the reaction of the people when I got to that point in the message. What a testimony to the conviction of the Holy Spirit *through* the Law.

Only two people (out of about 50–70) rejected the gospel during the week I was there. The first home I preached in, one couple broke down crying when I went through the Law. The woman was a witch, but she came to Christ. Another lady who was studying at the Seventh Day Adventist church broke down crying when I continued to press her, "Why would God let you, a sinner, into heaven on the Day of Judgment?" She yielded her life to Christ. Jehovah's Witnesses who came to Christ set up meetings with their friends within two days because they wanted their friends to hear the gospel presented to them. It was incredible.

Fortunately, some are seeing the necessity of returning to biblical evangelism. Following is a letter from a woman who had given her pastor a CD of "Hell's Best Kept Secret":

I kept praying and praying asking God to open a door. Today a huge answer to prayer came through in an even bigger way. After worship, the pastor got really quiet on the platform and tears started to well in his eyes. He said, "I don't know why I'm doing this, but when God tells me to do something and I don't do it, I'm disobeying him." He then asked the tech guy to queue up the video and for twenty minutes it was nothing but the Law: "Do you think you're a good person? Have you ever told a lie? What about ever cheating?"

Three hours later (we were there from 11:00–2:15), people all over the congregation were coming up confessing they had false conversions—deacons, nursery workers, people you would never have imagined! My eyes were filled with tears as I couldn't believe the miracle God was showing me right before my eyes. The pastor said he was tired of sugar-coating the gospel and that all of us will have to face judgment. He said that by not sharing he was keeping something vital from his congregants, and that God wouldn't let him rest until he spoke about the Law...God is moving huge here!

Jude knew that we must be "faultless before the presence of His glory" (verse 24). This is because we have a faultless God who will judge with a faultless Law, and we therefore must present every man faultless in Christ Jesus. It is obvious that this isn't the goal of many modern preachers. Those who don't fear God don't see that their commission is to pull sinners from the fire. There is no urgency in their words. There is no wrath of God to be feared. There is no need to present every man perfect in Christ. By what they teach their congregations, it would appear that all that matters to them is happiness and success in this life.

Listen to this wisdom of Spurgeon once again, as he speaks of preachers in his day, well before the rise of seeker-centered Christianity:

Sometimes we are inclined to think that a very great portion of modern revivalism has been more a curse than a blessing, because it has led thousands to a kind of peace before they have known their misery; restoring the prodigal to the Father's house, and never making him say, "Father, I have sinned." How can he be healed who is not sick? or he be satisfied with the bread of life who is not hungry? The old-fashioned sense of sin is despised, and consequently a religion is run up before the foundations are dug out. Everything in this age is shallow. Deep-sea fishing is almost an extinct business so far as men's souls are concerned. The consequence is that men leap into religion, and then leap out again. Unhumbled they come to the church, unhumbled they remained in it, and unhumbled they go from it.

If, like Jude, your passion is to present every man faultless before Christ, then expound the Law to bring the knowledge of sin, warning them of future punishment. Such preaching is the way of the Master, and works with the Holy Spirit to see true conversions.

As we have seen, Jesus, Paul, Stephen, Peter, James, John the Baptist, and Jude all used the Law lawfully, speaking about the reality of sin and its just consequences, in order to lead sinners to the cross. Now it's your turn to follow in the way of the Master. In the next chapter we will discuss practical ways you can use the principles of biblical evangelism as you witness for Christ.

Chapter Twelve

WHAT CAN *YOU* DO?

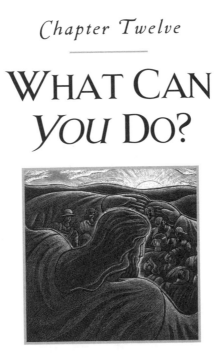

I hope that through these pages you have become convinced that much of the Church today has moved far away from biblical evangelism, instead offering Jesus as the ultimate Fixit-Man for humanity. Unto us a Child was born, unto us a Son was given—the Savior came to this world to save His people from their sins, but we have presented Him as the Wonderful Life Planner, the Great Marriage Counselor, the Mighty God-shaped Hole Filler, the Prince of Peace of Mind, and the Everlasting Father figure. We have added what we think is necessary to attract people to the message, and taken away what we think is offensive.

Perhaps you acknowledge that Jesus used the Law to bring the knowledge of sin, as did Paul and others, but you don't think it's really necessary today. So let's think through an example of how to reach someone using the modern gospel message, without incorporating the Law.

Imagine you have an opportunity to go back a few years and witness to Lance Armstrong, the world champion cyclist—just after the famous athlete was diagnosed with terminal cancer. Before you formulate your words, here is some insight into his life philosophy from his book *It's Not About the Bike:*

> The night before brain surgery, I thought about death. I searched out my larger values, and I asked myself, if I was going to die, did I want to do it fighting and clawing or in peaceful surrender? What sort of character did I hope to show? Was I content with myself and what I had done with my life so far? I decided that I was essentially a good person, although I could have been better, but at the same time I understood that the cancer didn't care.

> I asked myself what I believed. I had never prayed a lot. I hoped hard, I wished hard, but I didn't pray. I had developed a certain distrust of organized religion growing up, but I felt I had the capacity to be a spiritual person, and to hold some fervent beliefs. Quite simply, I believed I had a responsibility to be a good

person, and that meant fair, honest, hardworking, and honorable. If I did that, if I was good to my family, true to my friends, if I gave back to my community or to some cause, if I wasn't a liar, a cheat, or a thief, then I believed that should be enough. At the end of the day, if there was indeed some Body or presence standing there to judge me, I hoped I would be judged on whether I had lived a true life, not on whether I believed in a certain book, or whether I'd been baptized. If there was indeed a God at the end of my days, I hoped he didn't say, "But you were never a Christian, so you're going the other way from heaven." If so, I was going to reply, "You know what? You're right. Fine."[110]

In deciding that he was "essentially a good person," Lance's philosophy is typical of the world (see Proverbs 20:6). How are you going to witness to him? Perhaps you could simply share the Good News that Jesus died for his sins. *What sins?* He thinks that he's essentially a good person. Modern evangelism says that the lost don't need to be told about the nature of sin because they're already aware of it. But the Bible says that they aren't (see Romans 7:7), and Lance's words attest to that.

Notice where he went for his gauge of the moral standard required of him: "If I wasn't a liar, a cheat, or a thief, then I *believed* that should be enough." The work of the Law was written on his heart (see Romans 2:15). He knew

---

[110] Lance Armstrong, *It's Not About the Bike: My Journey Back to Life* (Penguin Putnam: 2000), pp. 112,113.

that some sort of "goodness" was required by God. When he considered facing Him in Judgment, he said, "I believed I had a responsibility to be a good person, and that meant fair, honest, hardworking, and honorable."

Then he said that if God was going to send him to hell for eternity, "Fine." His words show that he had no realistic fear of condemnation. Why? Because there was no way God could condemn him. After all, he was essentially a good person.

Behind his words is the attitude: "Okay, God. I'm a morally upright human being. If you are so unreasonable, so unjust, so unfair, then okay...send me to hell. I don't care." In other words, the thought of ending up in hell wasn't in the equation. Why? Because he was deceived into thinking that God's standards were the same as his.

Notice also that, like many people, he didn't want to use the name "hell," referring to it instead as "the other way from heaven." If even Christians can't bring themselves to speak of the reality of hell, why should we expect the world to take it seriously?

So, what will you say to Lance to show him that he needs the Savior? Perhaps you could say that God had a wonderful plan for his life. Then again, he's just been diagnosed with deadly cancer, so that doesn't fit. There's nothing wonderful about the way cancer is treated. The "cure" is often worse than the disease.

How about telling him that God will heal him—if he gives his heart to Jesus? But what if God chooses not to heal him? Then again, you know that Lance eventually ends up completely conquering the disease without giving his heart to Jesus.

How about telling him that he isn't really happy, that the bike riding he so loved and lived for—and those six consecutive Tour de France victories—didn't really satisfy him? Tell him that the fame and riches that came with his success, and his marriage to a beautiful, successful, megastar wife, didn't really make him happy. He's likely to think the opposite.

Then again, you could simply follow in the steps of Jesus and show Lance the true nature of sin, so that he will understand the necessity of the cross, and why he needs to repent and trust the Savior.

The Intellectual Whip

Let's say you are witnessing to Marvin Motormouth. He tells you that he doesn't believe in God. He thinks he's as good as any Christian. He is hiding under the safety of self-righteousness. He believes that evolution is a scientific fact and therefore doesn't believe in the Bible. He has so many arguments against the things of God that you feel intellectually whipped. And you are whipped—that is, if you fail to use the weapons that God has put at your disposal. Cannons always outgun whips. If you understand what God has given you in the Ten Great Cannons of His Law, whenever a sinner cracks an intellectual whip, you will quietly smile as you light the first fuse to destroy his defenses.

Mr. Motormouth is a *motormouth* for a reason. Unbeknown to you, he has been feeding his sinful heart on hardcore pornography. (Recent statistics reveal that more Americans feed on pornographic material than watch all sporting events combined.[111]) This caused him to so burn with lust that he has secretly committed adultery. (*USA Today* reported that fifty-one percent of married people in the U.S. admit to adultery.) That's why he is trying to justify himself.

Most of us are familiar with what is commonly known as a "lie detector." However, the lie detector doesn't really detect lies at all. A polygraph machine is actually a combination of medical devices that are used to monitor changes occurring in the human body. As a person is questioned about a certain event, the examiner looks to see how the individual's heart rate, blood pressure, respiratory rate, and perspiration rate change in comparison to normal levels. Fluctuations may indicate that the person is being deceptive, but exam results are open to interpretation by the examiner. This is because some people are excellent liars. They can control these bodily functions so that their deception isn't outwardly evident.

As Christians, we should never underestimate the power of the God-given human conscience. It is a *perfectly accurate* lie detector. Its work may not be detectable outwardly, but it certainly is evident on the heart. The Bible tells us,

---

[111] Quoted on "Sixty Minutes," November 23, 2003.

"The sin of Judah is written with a pen of iron; with the point of a diamond it is engraved on the tablet of their heart..." (Jeremiah 17:1). The Law doesn't miss the slightest transgression. The pen with which it writes is made of iron. It is resolute and will not compromise. Its diamond nib has cut its inscriptions deep into the tablet of the human heart.

Mr. Motormouth may have total control over his physical functions, but he has little control over the conscience. He may dull its voice within his mind, but he can never dull the record that it is keeping on the heart. It details every transgression against God's Law.

For this reason, Mr. Motormouth *knows* in his heart that he has done wrong. The work of the Law, written on his heart, stands like a stubborn and an uncompromising judge, pointing a reproving finger. His guilt causes him to try to cover his shame with self-justification. *His adamant arguments reveal this to you.*

So don't be discouraged by his mouth. Think of his heart. Like Felix the governor, his mouth is saying, "Go away," *but his heart is trembling in fear* (see Acts 24:25). When you speak using God's Law, you are shining a bright light past his mind, into the hidden recesses of his dark and sinful heart (see Proverbs 6:23; John 3:19,20).

So it doesn't matter that he says he doesn't believe the Bible. Contrary to common belief, salvation doesn't come through believing the Bible. If you think it does, take yourself back to a witnessing situation around 40 A.D. when the

Bible, as we know it, hadn't yet been compiled. There was no such thing as a printing press. Most people couldn't read anyway. What you have to communicate in your witness is the *spoken* message of the gospel, and this is what you should present to Mr. Motormouth. You don't need to convince him of the inspiration of the Bible, or about the fallacy of evolution, etc. You need only convince him of his need for the Savior, and you can do that (with God's help) by using a little reasoning (to the intellect) and a lot of the Law (directed at the conscience).

Therefore, reason with him about the fact that if God is good, He must punish evil. Then speak to his conscience. Use the Law to bring his sin out into the open. Show him that in the face of the Law, he is without hope because God's wrath abides on him (see John 3:36). He is like the woman caught in the act of adultery (discussed earlier in the book). She knew she had sinned, but the Law brought her secret sin out into the open. It stood above her in wrath, showing her how seriously God looked upon her transgression. It left her without hope of escape, at the feet of the Savior.

Mr. Motormouth is up the River Niagara without a paddle, and there is only one rope being thrown to him. If he wants to be saved from going over the falls of eternal wrath, he must take hold of the rope that God has provided. The more clearly he hears the thunder of the falls, the more he will desire and appreciate the rope.

The fact that Jesus is the only hope for salvation is offensive to those who have not been taught by the Law. But once a sinner has seen how desperate his situation is, he is no longer offended by the great truth, "Nor is there salvation in any other" (see Acts 4:12). It becomes the most welcome and wonderful news. The rope is of little value to him...until he understands where he is going to end up without it.

Putting the Principles into Practice

I pray that God has given you a desire to follow the way of the Master and do what Jesus did in the most important of issues—reaching the lost. So let's look at how to put into practice these principles of biblical evangelism. Let me begin by recounting a couple of witnessing encounters I've had, so you can see how easy it is.

When I'm witnessing to people, I often ask for their names. I then try to log it into my memory banks so that when I talk about their sin, I use their name. They can't see my motive for witnessing to them, but the personalizing of their name let's them know that I care about them as a human being.

Sometime ago, a huge truck arrived at our ministry to deliver products. As I went outside to direct it to the parking lot, I saw a woman walking toward me. Her name was Pat, and it was her husband, Robert, who was sitting in the driver's seat of the truck.

As it was being unloaded, I took a copy of my book *What Hollywood Believes* and a CD of the same title and knocked on the cab door of the massive 70-foot 18-wheeler. When Pat opened it, I asked if she wanted a book, and then signed it to her and Robert. Then I went around to the back of the vehicle and started to help with the unloading.

As the man lifted boxes, I called out, "Good work, Robert." He looked at me and then carried on working, probably wondering how I knew his name.

After the shipment was unloaded, he came to the warehouse door to have the delivery sheet signed. I thanked him, using his name once again. Robert looked like a trucker. He was a man who had been worn down by a life of physical work, and although he smelled of cigarettes he had a softness about him. I decided that I should witness to him.

As we slowly walked toward his vehicle, I said, "I gave Pat a book and a CD. It's a Christian book. Have you had a Christian background?"

"Baptist."

"Do you think that you are a good person . . . will you go to heaven when you die?"

"I think so."

"Let me ask you some questions. These really helped me. Have you ever told a lie?"

"Yes."

"What does that make you?"

"A liar."

"Have you ever stolen something?"

"Yes."

"What does that make you?"

"A thief."

"Have you ever used God's name in vain?"

"Yes."

"That's called blasphemy—using God's name as a cuss word. Now listen to this. This one will nail you—it did me. Jesus said, 'Whoever looks at a woman to lust for her has already committed adultery with her in his heart.' Have you ever done that?"

"Many times."

I looked him in the eye and said, "Robert, this is how God sees you: as a lying, thieving, blasphemous, adulterer at heart. If He judges you by the Ten Commandments on the Day of Judgment, will you be innocent or guilty?"

"Guilty."

"Will you go to heaven or hell?"

"Hell."

"Does that concern you?"

"It *really* concerns me."

He was obviously humbled by the Law, so I said, "Do you know what God did for you so that you wouldn't have to go to hell?"

"He died for our sins."

"That's right. Jesus suffered on the cross for you. He took your punishment upon Himself, and what you must do is repent and trust Him. Repentance is more than confessing your sins to God. It means to *stop* sinning. No more lying or stealing. No more lusting. You might think, 'How could I stop lusting? It's such a part of me.' Robert, when you are born again, it's radical. At one point you didn't exist, and suddenly God gave you life; you were *born* into this world. That was a radical change. When you are born again, it's just as radical. God gives you a new heart with new desires—desires to please Him. When do you think that you will get right with God?"

He looked at me and said, "Real soon."

I asked, "How about here and now? Do you want to pray?"

He replied that he did, so I asked him to give me his hand and to pray asking God to forgive him and placing his trust in Jesus. After he prayed, I then prayed for him right there on the sidewalk. It must have looked a little strange— me and a hardened trucker holding hands and praying as people walked passed us.

We went back to the warehouse and I gave him a copy of *The Evidence Bible*, a CD of "Hell's Best Kept Secret," and a copy of "Save Yourself Some Pain," a booklet that gives principles of growth for new Christians. I said, "It's been an important day for you, Robert."

He said, "I know it—thank you," and went on his way.

It's important to remember that not every witnessing encounter is as fruitful as my time with Robert. I was able to reap because someone else had sown seed. The following is another witnessing example where a seed was planted, even if we don't see immediate fruit. God has His timing.

This One Will Nail You

I can detect a telemarketer even before he speaks. The background noise, the delay, then the tone of voice give them away instantly. I heard, "Good evening. I'm representing *The Press Telegram...*"

I quickly said that I wasn't interested in getting the paper; I got my news from TV. After the caller launched into the standard reply for folks like me, I asked, "What's your name?"

"Greg."

"Have you had a good day?" He gave an enthusiastic thumbs up, insinuating that the day had been wonderful with people clamoring to subscribe to the wonderful paper. When I asked him if some people hung up in his ear, he confessed that they had.

"It's pretty horrible when that happens, isn't it?"

He agreed.

I then asked, "Greg, do you consider yourself to be a good person?"

Now, you may be thinking, *How can he suddenly inject that question into the conversation?* I do it because I have a clear agenda. (I also feel the freedom to be a little more assertive with telemarketers, because they have approached me and they want to keep me happy.) Think of yourself as a doctor, with a patient sitting in front of you who has a terminal disease. He will die if he isn't treated immediately, and you have the cure he needs. So what are you going to do—chat about the weather? No, your focus is on his disease and the cure you have for him. You very deliberately swing the conversation the way you want it to go. I have done this a thousand times and if it is done with a gentle firmness of tone, it is neither indiscrete nor rude. It is what Jesus did in John chapter 4; He quickly transitioned from natural things (water) to spiritual things (living water).

Since Greg replied that he considered himself to be a good person, I said, "Let's go through a few questions and see if that's true. Have you ever told a lie?"

"Yes."

"Have you ever stolen something, even if it was small?"

"Yes."

"Ever used God's name in vain?"

"Yes."

Then I said, "Greg, this one will nail you. Jesus said, 'Whoever looks at a woman to lust for her has already committed adultery with her in his heart.' Have you ever done that?"

He had.

"Do you think that you will be innocent or guilty on the Day of Judgment?"

He thought that he would be guilty, so I followed with, "Do you think you will go to heaven or hell?"

He became quiet for a moment and said, "I will find out when I get there."

I told him that we already know where he will go. "The Bible says, 'All liars will have their part in the Lake of Fire.' I don't want that to happen to you. Do you know what God did for you so that you wouldn't have to go to hell?"

He said that he didn't know, so I told him about the cross and his need for repentance and faith in Jesus. I was pleased that we had talked about how horrible it is to have someone hang up in your ear; that probably stopped him from hanging up in mine. I thanked him that he didn't do that, asked him if he had a Bible, and encouraged him to read it. End of call. Seed planted.

Do you think you have the confidence to say those things to someone on the phone? All it takes is a little knowledge and some practice. Besides, if you blow it, say, "I've got to go now." Then hang up, and try again another time. All you have lost is a little pride.

How to Do What Jesus Did

Let me show you a structure I have used for many years to present the Law and the gospel. Remember that to do as Jesus did—to seek and save the lost—you have to seek them. Rarely will they come to you. So as you are going about your day, learn to initiate spiritual conversations with people you encounter. I often begin by greeting a person warmly and handing him a gospel tract.[112] Tracts are great "ice-breakers," giving you an easy way to start a conversation with strangers and to get the gospel into their hands if they don't want to talk.

I usually say, "Did you get one of these?" That makes them think that they're missing out on something—and they are—and then I follow up by saying, "It's a gospel tract.

---

[112] We have dozens of tracts that are unique and humorous, and so appealing that lost people often ask for more. See our website at www.livingwaters.com.

Have you had a Christian background?" You could also say, "May I ask you an important question? Do you ever think about what's going to happen to you after you die?"

After bringing up the subject of the things of God, ask the person, "Would you consider yourself to be a good person?" Most will answer that they do, as Proverbs 20:6 tells us: "Most men will proclaim each his own goodness." Ask, "Do you think that you have kept the Ten Commandments?" Then gently go through the Law.[113]

After you have opened up the spiritual nature of the Commandments, ask, "If God judges you by the Ten Commandments on Judgment Day, do you think you will be innocent or guilty?" Then, "Do you think you will go to heaven or hell?"

Here's how to remember what you have just learned. Use the acronym WDJD (What Did Jesus Do):

W: Would you consider yourself to be a good person?

D: Do you think you have kept the Ten Commandments?

J: Judgment—If God judges you by the Ten Commandments on Judgment Day, do you think you will be innocent or guilty?

D: Destiny—Do you think you will go to heaven or hell?

---

[113] For more information on how to share your faith using the Law—and to watch "live" witnessing encounters—see "The Way of the Master" series, at www.livingwaters.com.

Go through these principles in your mind until they become second nature. Role-play with a friend. Practice what you preach. Usually when I witness, the responses I receive are very predictable. Most people admit their sins; some are self-righteous. They may say, even after admitting to lying, stealing, blasphemy, and lust, that they still think they are good. If that happens, try to muster a smile and say, "No, you aren't. By your own admission, you are a lying, thieving, blasphemous, adulterer at heart."

The Bible tells us to "convince, rebuke, and exhort" them with patience and doctrine. If this person dies in his sins, he will spend eternity in hell. So we can't be concerned with a fear of offending or even of angering him.

If the person says that he doesn't believe in hell, tell him that the electric chair still exists, even if the criminal doesn't believe it. Our beliefs don't change reality. *Reason* with him about the "goodness" of God. Ask if he thinks that God is good. Most people do. If God is good, should He punish a vicious criminal who raped and murdered a woman and was never brought to justice? Most will naturally agree that He should, if He is good. Then ask the person if he thinks God is good enough to also punish thieves, adulterers, liars, etc. Tell him that God is so good, He's even going to punish us for every idle word that we speak, and that His place of punishment is called "hell."

What if someone says that he's kept *all* of the Ten Commandments—that he's never lied, stolen, lusted, or blasphemed? You know he's not being honest with you, so ask if he's kept the *First* Commandment. He will probably state that he has, so ask, "What is it?" (More than likely, he won't know.) Explain, "It is, 'You shall have no other gods before me.' That means that you are commanded to love God above everything else. Have you *always* done that?"

If he claims that he has, say, "The Bible says that there is *none* who seeks after God. No one has kept the First of the Ten Commandments. So one of you is lying—either you or God—and the Bible says that it's *impossible* for Him to lie. So now you've not only been found to have broken the *First* of the Commandments, but you've broken the *Ninth* by lying, and the Bible says that all liars will have their part in the Lake of Fire. You're in big trouble."

If he answers that there are hypocrites in the Church, tell him that God promises to sort the genuine from the false on the Day of Judgment, and that each of us will give an account of *ourselves*, not of others.

If he denies God's existence, explain that creation is absolute proof that there's a Creator.[114] In the same way, a painting is absolute proof that there is a painter; a building is proof that there is a builder. You cannot have one without the other. However, don't stay too long in the intellect, the place of argument.[115] Get back to the conscience, the place

---

[114] See *God Doesn't Believe in Atheists* by Ray Comfort (Bridge-Logos Publishers).

[115] *The Evidence Bible* (Bridge-Logos Publishers) contains one hundred of the most commonly asked questions and objections to the Christian faith.

of the knowledge of right and wrong. Never forget that we do not wrestle against flesh and blood. This is a spiritual battle, so fight it with the spiritual weapons God has provided for this purpose: the Law, which He's written in the heart, and the conscience, which bears witness to its truthfulness and brings conviction of sin. Gently and firmly take control of the conversation; let the person speak, but don't let him sidetrack you. Remember, you are a doctor with an agenda—to convince the patient of the disease of sin so he will appreciate the cure.

As you speak with the lost, always be loving, kind, but obstinately uncompromising when it comes to the issue of sin. Tell them that the moral Law will be God's standard on Judgment Day, that God will bring their every work into Judgment, and that it's a fearful thing to fall into His hands. Keep an eye out for the encouraging "deer in the headlights" look, to tell you that you are heading in the right direction.

The Gift

Let me close this book by telling you about a very memorable incident in my life. On December 5, 2004, I turned fifty-five. A month earlier, a friend called from Texas and asked if he could fly to California to take my wife, Sue, and me to a "nice restaurant" for my birthday. It seemed a little strange, but I said that it would be fine. He also said he had a gift for me that he wanted to hand-deliver.

For the next month, Sue and I were trying to guess why he had to hand-deliver a gift. There was nothing in this world that I wanted or even needed. Kirk knew what the gift was, but he wouldn't tell me. He just said, "You will *never* guess what it is!"

Each weekday for the previous 20 months, my son-in-law, "EZ," and I preached the gospel to a line of people who stood outside the courthouse across the street from our ministry. These were different folks every day, from all walks of life. They had been charged with misdemeanor crimes and were waiting to see the judge. My Texas friend asked if he could come to hear the preaching and film it as well.

On Friday, December 3, about ten people crowded into my office to pray before we preached. These included another out-of-town friend who had come to hear the preaching; my two sons, Jacob and Daniel (who didn't normally come to hear us speak); a few other members of the staff; and, for some reason, the director/producer of our TV show who showed up with a shoulder camera. It seemed a little strange, but I didn't give it much thought. I had enough on my mind because in three minutes I would be preaching.

Moments later, I was standing in front of a crowd collecting my thoughts when my youngest son, Daniel (who was in his late 20s), said to me, "Don't worry about it, Dad. Jacob and I will take it from here."

I said, "Huh?"

He added, "Jacob and I will preach this morning. Why do you think all these people and these cameras are here?" He immediately walked toward the waiting crowd.

My Texas friend then stuffed a packet of tissues into my hand and walked off. I sat down and stared in unbelief as my son introduced himself to the crowd and began preaching.

I must explain something to you at this point. My wife was born in England. She is typically English—quiet and shy. She got that disposition from her parents, and my boys have inherited the same disposition. So for them to get up and preach open-air to strangers took a great deal of courage. Believe me, I know what it takes. The first time I ever stood up and preached open-air, I was terrified. But this was worse. I was alone when I preached for the first time. My sons had the added pressure of preaching in front of their dad (and their mom, who was watching from a distance), in front of members of our staff and with two cameras rolling. I was *very* nervous for them.

After Daniel had faithfully gone through the Commandments and the reality of Judgment Day, he said to the listening crowd, "I will now hand it over to my brother, Jacob, who will share the good news with you." Jacob then stepped forward and preached the gospel.

A month earlier, my Texas friend had called them and said that he had a gift in mind for their dad and wondered if they would be willing to help him give it to me. They both just about died when he asked them to preach open-air as a present to me, but immediately agreed to do it. Interestingly, both of them said that God had already been speaking to them about having more of a concern for the lost. As

I listened to them preach, I nearly burst with pride, and I did use the tissues to wipe away tears of joy.

Kirk was right. There was no way I could have guessed what the gift would be. This was infinitely better than a new car, a world trip, or a cash donation to our ministry. As we walked away from the courts, Jacob smiled and said, "After today, the rest of my life will be a piece of cake."

Here is my point. If my shy boys can open-air preach to strangers, *you can witness one-to-one.* Do it as a "gift" to your heavenly Father. *Present* your body as a present to God—"a living sacrifice, holy, acceptable to God, which is your reasonable service" (Romans 12:1). Let gratitude fuel you to reach out to the unsaved—those who will end up in hell if they die in their sins without the Savior.

Compel them to come in. Let urgency drive you. Do all you can to be the best you can, to reach as many as you can. And the most effective way to do that is to simply ask, "What did Jesus do?" And then do what Jesus did.

> *"Only by imitating the spirit and the manner of the Lord Jesus shall we become wise to win souls."*
> —Charles Spurgeon

For a complete list of books, tracts, videos, DVDs, CDs, and other resources by Ray Comfort, go to www.livingwaters.com; write to Living Waters Publications, P.O. Box 1172, Bellflower, CA 90706; or call 800-437-1893.